ISLANDS OF THE CARIBBEAN

HANS W. HANNAU

ISLANDS of the CARIBBEAN

Full-color photographs, with text, of

Jamaica · Haiti · Dominican Republic · Puerto Rico · The Virgin Islands (St.Thomas · St.Croix · St. John · Tortola) · Sint Maarten · Saba · St. Barthélemy · St. Kitts · Nevis · Antigua · Montserrat · Guadeloupe · Dominica Martinique · St. Lucia · Barbados · St.Vincent · Bequia · Grenada · Trinidad Tobago · Curaçao, Bonaire, Aruba · Cayman Islands

Distributed by

DOUBLEDAY & COMPANY, INC. GARDEN CITY, NEW YORK

TO ILSE, WHO INSPIRED THIS BOOK
                    HANS

Library of Congress Catalog Card Number 70–81031
All rights reserved by the publisher and author.
Wilhelm Andermann Verlag, Munich.
Printed in Germany. 169

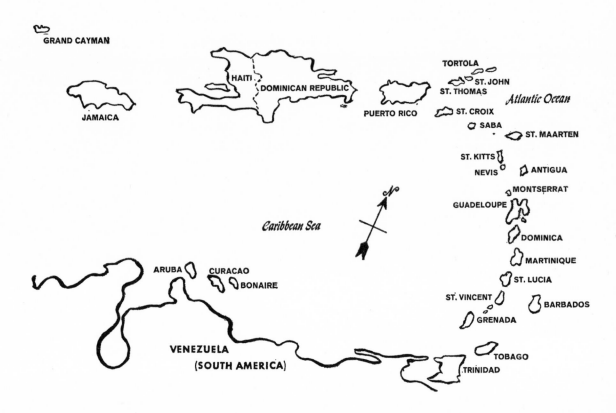

GRAND CAYMAN

HAITI · DOMINICAN REPUBLIC

JAMAICA

TORTOLA
ST. JOHN
ST. THOMAS
PUERTO RICO
ST. CROIX

Atlantic Ocean

SABA
ST. MAARTEN
ST. KITTS
NEVIS
ANTIGUA
MONTSERRAT
GUADELOUPE
DOMINICA
MARTINIQUE
ST. LUCIA
ST. VINCENT
BARBADOS
GRENADA

Caribbean Sea

ARUBA
CURACAO
BONAIRE

VENEZUELA
(SOUTH AMERICA)

TOBAGO
TRINIDAD

INTRODUCTION

For anybody who possesses a little imagination and a slight knowledge of the history of the New World, the entire Caribbean area has a magic all its own. Whether you look down upon a glittering and placid sea from your safe seat in a jet plane transporting you from Puerto Rico to Trinidad, or from the deck of an ocean liner en route from Miami to Jamaica and Haiti, you cannot help but feel that Time, our chronological annotation of days and years, has truly stopped. It would come almost as no surprise at all to see a British Fourmaster or a Spanish Galleon or a French Caravelle cutting across the horizon of the Spanish Main.

For the romantic history of the past four hundred years has thoroughly permeated this part of the world where Columbus and Cortés, Drake and De Soto, Ponce de León, Henry Morgan, Horatio Nelson, French buccaneers, English pirates, and Dutch privateers crossed and crisscrossed historic sea lanes in search of "the riches of the Indies" or, at least, new lands to conquer. The eye can almost visualize proud sails bearing the cross of the Spanish Catholic kings or the fleur de lys of Louis XIV of France or the insignia of Queen Elizabeth I of England.

But these have long since been replaced by giant steamships and giant airliners transporting tourists and businessmen, honeymooners and convention parties to the enchanted islands of the Caribbean.

This is the world of the American tropics, filled with glamor and romance. It has a wilder beauty than is known north of the Tropic of Cancer, and a climate that beckons one to a more langourous life. Nature has decorated the islands with a profusion of unfading greenery and colorful blossoms: orchid, flame vine, bougainvillea, hibiscus, morning-glory. The fruits bear exotic names — mango, avocado, papaya, guanabana, guava. The birds are numerous and colorful: the dove with iridescent plumage, the marvelous pink flamingo, the glittering hummingbird, the long-tailed doctorbird, the fruit finch or orangebird, the multicolored parrot and parakeet.

Consequently, the first appeal of the Caribbean islands is to the senses. The vivid colors of nature fascinate the eye; the taste is flattered by the luscious fruit; the ear is beguiled by the swish of palm fronds in the constant breeze; and the overall feeling of being caressed by the balmy air, seldom unbearably hot and almost never too cold, is a sensuous one.

Because of the unflagging interest that England, France, Spain, Holland, and Denmark displayed for four centuries in obtaining control of the islands, the cultural background is often multinational. Some islands changed hands among the European powers almost as quickly as it took the ink to dry on assorted treaties of peace. Today, of course, Great Britain maintains connections with a majority of the islands. The United States, through purchase and treaty concession, is the second Caribbean power. It possesses Puerto Rico (Spanish in origin and language) and more than 50 of the Virgin Islands, which it purchased from Denmark. France comes third, with sovereignty over Martinique, Guadeloupe, and assorted smaller islands. Holland's possessions include the islands of Curaçao and Aruba, where some of the world's greatest oil refineries are situated, as well as the islands of Bonaire, Sint Maarten, Saba, and St. Eustatius. Two independent countries, owing allegiance to no foreign power and forming no part of the British Commonwealth of Nations, are Haiti and the Dominican Republic.

Underlying the European civilization that conquest and settlement bestowed on these islands of eternal spring is the great primitive African culture drawn to this new world by the slave trade of past centuries. In many of the islands, descendants of those who experienced the horrors of the Middle Passage are predominant.

The islands of the Caribbean, in comparatively recent years, have begun to exploit the possibilities of what may become their main source of income: tourism. Since they possess what naturally attracts the foreign visitor — unsurpassed natural beauty, fascinating cities, historic monuments and sites of interest, magnificent beaches, blended cultures, hotels that range from the ultraluxurious to the quaintest beach accommodation, and the most salubrious and beneficial climate, particularly for the winter sojourner — it is no wonder that thousands of North and South Americans and Europeans travel far to reach these sunny islands.

6

Vikings landed on the North American continent some centuries before Columbus arrived in the New World, and Mongols, with dogs at their heels, came from Asia to Alaska many millennia before 1492 and drifted down the Americas to Patagonia. There is evidence of other voyages between the hemispheres. But all those earlier voyages remained unheralded and even unknown in Europe.

Columbus made sure that all Europe heard about the lands he found, even though he was faulty as a geographer. When he landed on San Salvador, a small island in the eastern Bahamas, he believed he was in Japan and that Cathay lay nearby. He was a competent navigator, however, making four trips between Spain and the colonies he established in the West Indies. But the great thing about him was that he was a believer and a doer.

A lookout on the *Pinta*, smallest of Columbus's three ships, shouted "Tierra! Tierra!" on October 12, 1492. When Columbus came ashore and saw the brown-skinned people who lived on the island, he called them "Indians." The Arawaks occupied the greater islands in the Caribbean at that time, and all Spanish accounts agree that they were a gentle, friendly, peaceful people. They did not need to be fierce hunters to capture their principal prey, the iguana and the aguti (a rodent). Fishing was more important to them, and mounds of conch shells testified to their taste for shellfish. They grew maize and made bread from cassava. They raised tobacco and used it as a drug, in rituals and in barter. Their pottery was attractive and they wove serviceable baskets. Their chief contribution to European culture was the hammock, which they wove from long-staple sea-island cotton and which was much admired by sailors.

The gentle Arawaks were soon to be extinct. Other Indians were pushing north from South America along the lesser Antilles, all the way to Puerto Rico, in their long dugout canoes. They were a fierce and warlike tribe, whom the Arawaks called "Carib," the word meaning "cannibal" in the Arawak language. The Caribs killed and enslaved the Arawaks as they came. After a few clashes with these fierce fellows, the Spaniards left the Caribs alone.

Columbus spent three days on San Salvador and then sailed south through the Bahamas in the direction in which the Indians indicated he might find the source of the few little gold ornaments they wore. Past many of the Bahama islands he sailed, going ashore briefly from time to time, until he reached what is now Oriente Province in Cuba. There, he wrote, "The little birds sing with much sweetness."

From Cuba he crossed to the large island he named Hispaniola, later to be divided between Haiti and the Dominican Republic. There he cruised along its northern coast and was given a little gold by Arawak Indians who called themselves Tainos. On Christmas day the *Santa Maria* went aground, and the first settlement in the New World was made. Columbus built a fort, left thirty-nine of his men there on Hispaniola, pledged the profits of his voyage to the conquest of the new Jerusalem, and returned to Spain aboard the *Niña*, accompanied by the *Pinta*.

Columbus's second voyage was made for the purpose of colonizing, and he had many volunteers. He left Cadiz in September 1493 with seventeen ships loaded with agricultural stock, tools, seeds, animals, and twelve hundred people. They included priests, farmers, artisans, and soldiers, lured by his lyrical description of the land and waters he had found. Crossing the Atlantic in twenty-one days, he made a good voyage and reached the northern coast of Hispaniola. There he found that the settlement of Navidad, where he had left his men on the first voyage, had been wiped out. He made a second settlement, Isabela, on the same coast, but it never thrived.

Sailing on, he explored the south coast of Cuba and discovered Jamaica. When he returned to the new settlement, he found that the colonists had already succeeded in provoking the peaceful Indians to war. The Spanish soldiers hunted them down with dogs and guns and enslaved the survivors. In 1496 Columbus's brother Bartolomé led the settlers to the south coast of Hispaniola, a healthier and much better site, and founded the town of Santo Domingo, which was to be the capital of the Spanish Indies for fifty years.

Columbus returned to Spain in the same year. He was again fitted out with a fleet, for further exploration, though he had few volunteers when he set out on that third voyage in 1498. He discovered the island of

Trinidad and the many mouths of the Orinoco river in Venezuela, where he first landed on the continent of South America. When he sailed back to Santo Domingo he found the settlers split into two factions. He tried to pacify them by doling the Indians out as slaves among both factions. Malcontents went back to Spain and reported him as a tyrant. The Spanish king sent Francisco de Bobadilla to supersede him, and Columbus was sent home in chains.

The Crown exonerated Columbus, gave him a handsome gift of two thousand ducats, and allowed him to make one more voyage. It was an easy trip, a twenty-one-day crossing of the Atlantic, and Martinique was his landfall. Thence he stopped briefly at Dominica and sailed past St. Croix and across the south coast of Puerto Rico. Off southern Hispaniola a great hurricane struck his little fleet. The four ships he commanded rode out the storm safely, and he continued westward to an island just off Honduras. He cruised along the coast of Central America, finding many Indians wearing gold ornaments. Because of the meat shortage they were eating sharks.

After battling with the Indians and losing a ship, the Admiral withdrew to Jamaica. There he ran his ships aground in 1503 and was marooned. A group of Spaniards and Indians made the dangerous crossing from Jamaica to Hispaniola in two canoes to bring rescuers. Finally, Columbus, in his fifty-third year, sailed for Spain in 1504. There he lived, a rich man, until his death two years later. His wish was to be buried in Hispaniola, and his body was buried in the cathedral at Santo Domingo.

The Spaniards mined gold on Hispaniola in the first two decades of the sixteenth century, but production fell off sharply after that. They raised great herds of cattle and pigs and panned alluvial gold in the streams. They became the first cowboys of the Western World. Because leather was highly valued at the time in Europe, the hides of cattle were more important than the beef. Oranges, lemons, figs, and bananas were introduced from Europe. Sugar, which was to shape the destiny of the Caribbean, was introduced into Hispaniola and the first sugar mill built there in 1508. (Sugar must be milled within forty-eight hours of the time it is cut.)

The Spaniards began to settle Jamaica in 1509, but they never considered the island important. They circumnavigated Cuba in 1508, and it proved to be an island, not a continent as Columbus had claimed. Settle-

ment began in 1511, under Diego Velázquez, who founded seven towns, all of which survive today. Santiago was at first the most important city in Cuba, but with the development of trade routes to the Spanish mainland, Havana later became the island's chief city. Ponce de León was the first governor of Puerto Rico and made an unsuccessful try at settling that island in 1514. Because the Caribs resisted fiercely, few Spaniards colonized Puerto Rico in the sixteenth century.

With the discovery of gold in Mexico by Balboa and in Peru by Pizarro, the islands of Hispaniola and Cuba became the bases for the conquest of the continent. All the ships that carried flour, oil, wine, goods, and slaves from Seville to Mexico and Peru passed through the Caribbean, and fleets loaded with precious metals headed home to Spain by way of the Florida channel north of Havana. For a little while the islands were protected from the attention of other nations because they were so remote. But soon the stream of ocean-borne commerce and Spanish gold attracted the attention of other Europeans. From about 1530, pirates, privateers, and smugglers from France, Holland, and England began to swarm to the Caribbean. The Spanish colonists welcomed the smugglers, who sold to them the slaves and other things they needed more cheaply than did their own Spanish merchants, but they lived for several centuries in fear of the pirates and the privateers.

For a century after Columbus discovered the West Indies, no other European nation attempted to colonize any of the islands. At the end of the sixteenth century the Dutch began to mine salt in Venezuela. The English tried to settle the Guiana coast in 1604. The first permanent English settlement in the Caribbean was made on St. Kitts (St. Christopher) in the Leeward Island chain in 1624. The Dutch, bitter enemies of Spain, organized the West India Company, a great joint-stock corporation that made its profit by alternately plundering Spanish and Portuguese colonies and trading with them. They brought slaves to the West Indies, bought tobacco grown there. Between 1630 and 1640 the Dutch took Curaçao, Saba, St. Martin, St. Eustatius, and Aruba, all small islands, which they used chiefly as trading bases. These islands are today the Netherlands Antilles.

Shortly after the English settled on St. Kitts, a French colony was established there too. The English next claimed Barbados, with its fine forests and fertile soil. St. Croix in the Virgin Islands was settled jointly by the English and Dutch. The British came to Antigua and Montserrat to stay in 1632. The French colonized Martinique and Guadeloupe in 1635. On the early plantations of these islands, cotton and tobacco were the only important crops. The white population of the British West Indies reached its peak in the 1640s and has declined since then. Jamaica was captured formally from the Spaniards by an English naval operation in 1655, in a British expedition designed to gain control of the West Indies seaways. There were only about 1,500 Spanish settlers raising cattle on the island at that time, and England went to war with Spain to keep possession of Jamaica. The French settled Saint-Domingue on Hispaniola.

Though sugar was introduced in the Caribbean islands early in the sixteenth century, the sugar revolution that brought the West Indies their greatest prosperity did not really begin to peak until a hundred years later. The demand for sugar in Europe was great. The Dutch brought the cane to the French and British West Indies in the 1640s and taught the colonists there the secrets of sugar making. After 1650, sugar cane was the principal crop of the islands and led to vast plantations and a great demand for slaves. In Barbados in 1640, for example, there were only a few hundred Negroes. By 1685 there were 46,000 Negroes and 20,000 whites. Increasingly, a small number of white planters bought up smaller holdings and ruled a large Negro labor force.

Competition among the sugar-producing islands was keen. The wars of Europe continued to plague the Caribbean throughout the seventeenth century, and during peacetime pirates prevented true peace. It was trade in the West Indies that prompted England to go to war repeatedly against Spain and France between 1739 and 1763. A large English fleet attacked the Spanish West Indies and the Spanish Main in 1740. The operation dislocated trade, though it failed to capture any important city. England and France went to war in 1744 over the bitter rivalry between their sugar colonies. A squadron of English warships was permanently stationed in the Caribbean, with naval bases at Antigua and Jamaica during the war. The contestants were quite simply trying to wreck each other's colonies and put them out of the sugar-producing business.

After a brief peace, the Seven Years' War between the French and the English broke out in 1756 and raged from the West Indies to Canada and to India. Spain entered the war in 1762. England ended the war tremendously in ascendancy as to colonies all over the world. Yet, at the Treaty of Paris in 1763, England returned Cuba to Spain and Martinique to France, after having captured them in battle, and so threw away the last chance to unite the West Indies. In return for giving back the islands, England under the treaty was granted vast lands on the continent – Canada and Florida.

After the peace treaty at Paris, where the French lost Louisiana and Canada, the French West Indies entered a golden age. The French islands became the principal sugar exporters, outdoing the British, who had profited so much between the two preceeding wars. The Dutch islands of Curaçao and St. Eustatius became prosperous clearing houses for trade, and ships of many nations put into their fine free ports.

When war broke out again, between Great Britain and her thirteen rebellious colonies in North America in 1776, the West Indians had to choose sides. They knew they needed the Royal Navy to defend the islands, and though they had some sympathy with the American rebels they did not join them. France and Spain jumped into the fighting and plundered the British islands in the Caribbean. There was much fierce fighting in the British West Indies. After the American colonies achieved independence and the United States was born, the British islands in the Caribbean suffered from the loss of trade with North America, because Great Britain forbade it. After the American Revolution, cotton of fine quality grown in the Leeward Islands and sold to British mills became a major source of revenue. Two new trees were introduced into the Caribbean about that time, the ackee tree from West Africa and the mango tree from Asia.

In the latter years of the eighteenth century, a vast army of slaves was supporting a favored few whites on large plantations. There was a sharp distinction between the mulattoes, who frequently were free, and the black slaves. The population of the free mulattoes and creoles grew, and with it grew resentment at restrictions imposed by the whites on "people of color" even though they were free. A "spirit of subversion" was in the air on the eve of the French Revolution.

It was in French Saint-Domingue that the explosion began. In August, 1791, African drums began sending the message of revolt across the northern plains in what is now Haiti, and the slaves rose in all their might, killing whites and burning cane fields. It was the first big slave revolt in the West Indies. There were twenty times as many slaves as there were white people. In the western part of Saint-Domingue, mulattoes and whites fought. France dispatched Jacobin troops, who, in the name of the principals of the French Revolution, fought on the side of the revolting slaves. France emancipated the slaves, and Spain and England went to war against France. White French colonists fled.

François-Dominique Toussaint (soon to be called Toussaint L'Ouverture) was the first of the remarkable Haitian military leaders. He built up a force of about four thousand effective Negro troops and fought on the side of the army of France. Toussaint's forces first expelled English troops attacking the island and then defeated the mulatto faction that had been warring in the west and south. He was supreme within the colony by 1800. He drew up a remarkable constitution in 1801, which had a modern ring even though he proclaimed himself governor-general for life. Napoleon thereupon sent an army to reduce Toussaint to obedience. The black hero was captured and died in a French prison.

Jean Jacques Dessalines, an African-born slave, took over the forces Toussaint had headed. In 1804 he proclaimed himself Emperor of Haiti, choosing the Taino word "Haiti," which means "mountainous," to replace the name of Saint-Domingue. He died in 1806 and was followed by the giant Negro Henri Christophe, who built himself a great citadel in the north and ruled there until his death in 1820. Pétion, a mulatto leader, dominated the southern part of Haiti, where land was divided into small peasant plots.

The maroons (fugitive slaves and the free descendants of slaves) of Jamaica and the Caribs of St. Vincent staged a desperate outbreak against the English in 1795. The slave trade was abolished between 1804 and 1820 by Denmark, Britain, Sweden, Holland, France, and Spain, though Cuba was importing slaves up to 1865. The 1820s saw outbreaks of slaves in Barbados and Jamaica, and in 1831 the slaves again rose violently in the western part of Jamaica. Finally, in 1833, slavery was abolished in the British West Indies, and in 1848 in the French colonies. To Trinidad, which had a very small population when England took over that island in the Napoleonic wars, many free "persons of color" and many white refugees from Saint-Domingue came in the first half of the nineteenth century.

The years following the end of slavery saw the slow collapse of one world and the beginning of the building of a new one. On some islands the transition between being a slave and being a peasant proprietor of a small landholding was not too hard or slow. On others the laborers became wage slaves. Plantations crumbled. The sugar industry collapsed, except in Cuba. There was a flight of labor from the estates and a flight of capital and of white owners from many of the islands. However, the nineteenth century also saw new waves of immigration to the Caribbean. Planters in both the British and Spanish West Indies made a determined effort to recruit labor from the mother countries, with some success. East Indian laborers were recruited over a period of eighty years to work as indentured laborers on the plantations. Almost half a million people came from Asia to the West Indies.

At first, after the slaves were freed in the British colonies, total political apathy settled upon them, to be followed by violent passions and bitter animosities. Crown colony government in the latter half of the nineteenth century put an end to bickering and was paternal and impartial. As a makeshift, to bridge a gap to the representative government of the twentieth century, it performed usefully in some fields, such as public works.

The French West Indies took a different course after slavery was ended there. After the French Revolution of 1848, the colonies were granted elected representation in the National Assembly of France. The remnants of the French American empire—Martinique, Guadeloupe, and Cayenne—each elected three representatives to the National Assembly; they were usually colored, though no less French for being so. Thus the French West Indies were on their way more than a century ago to being what they are today, a department of France. They remain today devotedly French in culture, more strongly bound than ever to France politically.

At the end of the eighteenth century there were only three Spanish colonies in the West Indies—Santo Domingo, Cuba, and Puerto Rico. Santo Domingo had become a sleepy land of great estates that raised many cattle and a little sugar. When the slaves took over neighboring Saint-Domingue and renamed it Haiti, they swarmed across the border. Santo Domingo fell under the rule of Haiti until 1844, and the period bred a mutual hostility between the two peoples that still erupts occasionally. Mulattoes largely ruled in the new Dominican Republic after the Haitians were expelled in 1844. The country was very poor. Spain reoccupied it in 1861 but withdrew, simply because it was an unprofitable land to hold. A time of anarchy was followed by tyranny. Ulises Heureaux became a dictator for eighteen years. Brave, vindictive, and corrupt, he was assassinated in 1899. The country was bankrupt and in chaos.

Cuba's life in the nineteenth century was in sharp contrast. The island was larger and richer and had people with a better education and a prideful cultural heritage. Small farms raised fine tobacco. Sugar production increased dramatically. White immigration mounted. Political disorganization in Spain grew during the century, and with it the movement to free Cuba. Those moving for separation from Spain were white creoles in Cuba, angered because their lives were controlled from afar. Spain sent out captain-generals who were martinets to suppress all separatist activity in Cuba, the last colony offering wealth and patronage to the mother country. Slave revolts broke out and there was a strong revulsion against the slave trade. President Polk of the United States made an offer to Spain to buy Cuba in 1848, but it was turned down.

Carlos Manuel de Céspedes, lawyer, landowner, and liberal, became a leader of the Cubans who wanted independence. He freed his slaves and with his followers declared the independence of Cuba at Yara in 1868. The Ten Years War followed. Céspedes, who died in it, is a national hero to this day. The war crippled the economy. The creation of the American Sugar Refining Company in the United States in 1890 hurt it even more. With this company, the "Sugar Trust," controlling distribution of sugar in the United States, the price of sugar to growers dropped and dropped again. U.S. tariffs on sugar and tobacco under McKinley were also crippling to Cuba.

It was in this period that José Martí, one of the most magnetic and able visionaries of the West Indies, assumed the role of leadership of the Cuban Junta and raised the banner of revolt in 1895. Crops and buildings were burned, atrocities occurred on both sides. The United States went to war against Spain in 1898 when the battleship *Maine* was sunk by an explosion on a "courtesy visit" to Havana harbor. The United States won the war quickly. American government in the island followed for three years. Its prime accomplishment was proof by a team of American and Cuban physicians that mosquitoes carry yellow fever. This led to the development of a vaccine and the dawn of a new era in the Caribbean. The United States did not annex Cuba, though there was some sentiment for the move, but did annex Puerto Rico and did obtain Guantánamo as a naval base in Cuba.

To some of the Caribbean islands the twentieth century has brought a good new day, to others it has been as stormy as all the previous centuries since Columbus arrived. The Dutch islands have thrived magnificently. Two of the world's largest oil refineries, which refine Venezuelan oil, have been built on Aruba and Curaçao because of the stable political climate and the fine harbors. The tourist-resort attractions that have been built are modern and luxurious. The Netherlands Antilles are autonomous members of the Dutch kingdom and very happy in the relationship. Aruba has no illiteracy and does have the third-highest standard of living in the western hemisphere, with cradle-to-the-grave social security. Aruba has the world's largest plant for distilling fresh water from the sea. Fine vegetables, enough to feed the island and export a surplus, are raised on a modern hydroponic farm.

Puerto Rico was one of the poorest of the Spanish colonies and remained so for many years after it became a United States possession. The island began to emerge from apathetic poverty after World War II under the leadership of the astute Luis Muñoz Marín. Today it is a shining example to other Caribbean islands of what can be done in courting tourism, industry, and investment. It throbs with pride and progress, and there is a strong movement today for Puerto Rico to become the fifty-first of the United States.

After a series of rightist dictators, Cuba has worked out its destiny since 1958 under Fidel Castro, who proclaims himself a friend of communism. Thousands of refugees leave for Florida every month. A takeover by communists in the Dominican Republic was prevented by United States intervention in 1966, the last of several twentieth-century United States interventions in that country to quiet chaos and stop bloodshed. In Haiti, the United States also intervened, in 1915, when anarchy threatened. The occupation, though it brought order and material improvements, was deeply resented. It ended in 1934 with President Roosevelt's enunciation of his "good neighbor" policy. Since then Haiti has been comparatively peaceful.

In the 1930s the British colonies obtained universal suffrage and in the 1950s new constitutions with systems of ministerial responsibility. Foreign relations and defense remain the responsibility of the United

Kingdom. The internal government is of the people, by the people, and for the people, with eventual political independence in the offing. Following the wreckage of the short-lived British West Indian Federation, these islands are learning to cope with independence, and today in the British West Indies the pulse of change and progress beats strong.

SLAVERY

Negro slavery was first generally introduced into the West Indies in 1515, as a result, in part, it is said, of the efforts of a Spanish Dominican missionary, Bartolomé de Las Casas. Born in Seville in 1474, Las Casas visited the West Indies with his father at the age of nineteen. At that time he found that the native Indians were being divided among the Spanish settlers as slaves of their conquerors. Dominican priests hurled curses from the pulpit upon the heads of those who were exterminating the Indians through hard labor and ill treatment under this system.

Las Casas was incensed and took the cause of the Indians to King Ferdinand, who expressed deep compunction for his guilt in authorizing the system that caused so much suffering and destruction among innocent people. However, Ferdinand died without doing anything about it. He was followed by Charles V of Germany, who appointed Cardinal Ximenes as his regent. The cardinal set up a commission of monks who reported that the Spaniards must either give up their American conquests or be satisfied with very little gain unless the system of slavery was to be tolerated.

Therefore, to protect the Indians, Las Casas at last thought of introducing Negroes from Africa into the West Indies to do the work, it is said by some historians. He reasoned that the Portuguese were using their African lands to capture the inhabitants and sell them as slaves anyway. The Negroes were stronger, more hardy, less primitive, and more adaptable than the Indians. Charles V listened to this line of reasoning and granted a favorite courtier a patent empowering him to purchase slaves in Africa and ship them to the West Indies. It is to the credit of Cardinal Ximenes that he strongly protested the propriety of condemning one innocent people to slavery to save another. Some say there is no evidence that the Dominican missionary Las Casas, who wrote *The Brief Relation of the Destruction of the*

Indies and devoted his life to protecting the Indians, is guilty of having substituted African slaves. However, many Spaniards who protected the Indians saw nothing inconsistent in Negro slavery.

The native Indians were almost entirely exterminated throughout the Caribbean in spite of this measure, for their conquerors often drove the Caribs off their islands. An old historian wrote, "Fire and sword came among them, and the ancient people of the soil are no more."

The favorite courtier who had been granted a monopoly on the slave trade to the Spanish colonies immediately sold his patent to some Genoese merchants, who began the slave trade. For many years, this bloodstained commerce belonged exclusively to the Portuguese and Genoese. The Dutch then entered the profitable business. It was in 1564 that the first Englishman to do so, John Hawkins, later Sir John, carried on the traffic. It is said that before he died he was impressed with the horror of what he had done in violating the laws of humanity.

A few stories told of slaves have a happy ending. The Negro Juan de Parega was sent from the West Indies as a present to Diego Velázquez, the celebrated Spanish painter, about the year 1600. Juan, who was very talented, studied painting, but in secret, because he felt that his master might become angry. Philip the Fourth of Spain, an admirer of the fine arts, made one of his frequent visits to the studio of Velázquez when the painter was absent. He asked to see a painting that had been turned to the wall by Juan. The king studied it, called it beautiful. The slave fell to his knee, admitted he had painted it, apologized for his presumption, and asked His Majesty to intercede with Velázquez for the slave's pardon. Velázquez not only pardoned him, he freed him and the Negro became one of the leading portrait painters of his day.

Slavery was almost never thus, and the institution was hardly more brutalizing to the slaves than to their masters. Consider the Negro slave who was flayed by his master, thrown into a dungeon, and died there five days later, for the crime of eating a mango that fell off a tree he was watching. The tales of brutal cruelty on the part of slaveowners are more numerous and more repellent than the accounts of the slaves' revolts.

When sugar cane became the major crop in the islands, slavery became even more indispensable, it was thought, and the commerce of supplying slaves to the islands became second in importance to the sugar trade

12

itself. Five nations were involved: Portugal, England, France, Holland, and Spain. The first four obtained slaving bases in West Africa, where Negroes were rounded up in barracoons on the beaches for sale to slavers. Spain, which had by far the largest colonies in the New World, never actually got a foothold on the African coasts until late in the history of the abomination, and was largely a customer of the slave traders.

Spain in 1595 arranged *asientos,* whereby the slave trade was let to contractors who paid license fees to the king and obtained slaves through the Portuguese in Lisbon. The Dutch moved in as slave "smugglers," breaking down the monopoly. English planters in Barbados and the Leeward Islands began planting sugar and buying Negroes from the Dutch in the midseventeenth century, though it was illegal under British law to buy from the Dutch. To avoid such illegality, the Royal Africa Company was incorporated in England in 1672, principally to supply the English West Indies with slaves at the price of seventeen pounds (one ton of sugar) per slave. In Africa they could be bought at about three pounds per person at that time. Before long the English government decided that slaving was not just a means of supplying labor to grow sugar, but was a profitable mercantile pursuit in itself.

By the end of the seventeenth century, the French had taken over the Dutch slave trade and were transporting most of the slaves to the Spanish colonies from Senegal. In the War of the Spanish Succession, which ended in 1713, the concession of the slave trade by Spain to France was an important bone of contention. The English and the Dutch found this one reason to go to war against Spain and France. As a result of the Treaty of Utrecht, which ended that war, the English took the slave concession away from the French and organized the South Sea Company for trading rights in Spanish America. Brief wars followed, disrupting all Caribbean trade throughout the last years of the century.

In 1749 an English pamphlet defending the slave trade said: ". . . and the daily Bread of the most considerable Part of our British Manufacturers are owing primarily to the Labour of Negroes, who, as they are the first happy instruments of raising our Plantations: So their Labour only can support them and preserve them and render them still more and more profitable to their Mother-Kingdom." The evils of slavery drove the prosperous and more or less decent planters in Jamaica and the French colony on Saint-Domingue away to Europe to live on the proceeds of their plantations, when they began to have proceeds. By 1800, English slave ships were boasting when they brought in a slave cargo without one human dead. The usual rate, among both slaves and crew, was about twenty-five percent.

The first powder keg of slavery to explode was France's Saint-Domingue, the French colony on Hispaniola that is now Haiti. During the French Revolution, between 1788 and 1791, the landowners sent representatives to the meetings of the Estates General and openly defied the French revolutionary government. They sought "liberty," they said, but it was liberty to control their own slavery-based world. However, in France the Amis des Noirs, an antislavery group nurtured on the *Rights of Man,* had been founded. In 1791 the French National Assembly decreed that persons of color, if otherwise qualified in every aspect and born of free parents, should have the right to vote. The white rulers in the French Caribbean colonies refused to enforce the law.

In August 1791 the slaves of the north in Saint-Domingue rose in revolt and went forth burning houses and murdering whites. There were about 10,000 whites, 200,000 slaves. White, black, and mulatto warred against one another. A Jacobin army sent out from France in 1792 fought on the side of the revolting slaves for liberty, equality, and fraternity. In 1793 emancipation was proclaimed. Spain and England invaded Saint-Domingue. A maroon war broke out in Jamaica. Then came the series of remarkable Negro leaders in Haiti, mentioned earlier: Toussaint, Dessalines, and the mighty Negro slave Henri Christophe. Then it was that the French colonial slaves in Haiti freed themselves and formed an independent republic.

Abolition in the British colonies began at home, in England, with the profound revulsion of the Quakers toward slavery. The industrial revolution getting under way in England made the income from the British West Indies sugar-producing colonies of less importance. In 1772 the chief justice of England held that, in the absence of positive law on the subject, the right of property in slaves could not be upheld in England. This immediately liberated about 10,000 West Indian slaves who had been taken to England.

William Wilberforce, witty, wealthy, and eloquent, became converted to the Quaker faith and devoted his life to abolishing the slave trade and slavery. The slave trade was banned by Great Britain in 1808, with the missionaries bringing pressure to bear. There were slave riots in Barbados, Jamaica, and Guinea in the 1820s. Slaves rose violently in Jamaica in 1831. Finally the Emancipation Law was passed in 1833 and slaves were freed in all British colonies. Fifteen years later they were freed in all the French colonies, when slavery was abolished forever by France in 1848.

By the middle of the nineteenth century there were no more slaves in the West Indies except in the Spanish islands. When French Saint-Domingue had erupted early in the century, the violence spilled over into Spanish Santo Domingo, today the Dominican Republic. The hostility between those two nations that was born in those times still remains. Both countries slipped into anarchy alternating with dictatorship.

Cuba was the last of the larger islands in which slavery was banned. It had a big open trade in slaves after 1791. Sugar and pig plantations thrived. By 1817 the census showed whites in a minority. In a population of 630,000, there were 291,000 whites, 224,000 slaves, and 115,000 free "persons of color." Observing these figures, the white minority passed laws that proved successful in courting white European immigration to the island. The slave trade was banned in Cuba in 1817, but not effectively halted until 1865. Provision was finally made for the emancipation of slaves in Cuba in 1880, and they were finally freed in 1886.

THE PIRATES AND THE BUCCANEERS OF THE SPANISH MAIN

First there was gold being carried over the sea and then there were sea robbers, almost from the beginning of recorded time, in the Mediterranean Sea. "Viking" means pirate in old Norse. Though piracy did not originate in the Caribbean, no part of the world ever bred a crop of pirates that were bolder, fiercer, crueler, or more legend-encrusted than did this beautiful sea. Gold-laden galleons sailed well-known seaways from the Spanish Main (the mainland of Central and South America) back to Spain. They carried emeralds, too, bezoar stones from Guayaquil, and silver by the ton.

Less than fifty years after Columbus discovered America, pirates were raiding the Spanish galleons.

The Spaniards had found little gold in the Caribbean islands, and it was not until Hernando Cortés reached Mexico in 1519 and Francisco Pizarro claimed Peru for Spain in 1531 that the vast treasures of gold, of which the conquistadors had for so long dreamed, materialized. Spain had four great mining centers—two in what is now Mexico and was then New Spain; the fabled Potosí mine in Bolivia, then part of the viceroyalty of Peru, and one in Peru. High-sided galleons armed with cannons lumbered home under great square sails and with huge cargoes. By 1537 Spain was guarding these treasure fleets with men-of-war because of the Barbary pirates in the Mediterranean and others that were appearing in the West Indies.

The pope had divided the world in half in 1493, giving to Portugal all the non-Christian countries east of a certain line and to Spain all those west of that line. The Protestant nations of Europe did not recognize the validity of the division, and they too were colonizing in the New World. Nowhere did they find gold in such vast quantities as that produced by the mines of the Spaniards.

Spain's enemies in Europe spawned the first privateers and pirates. There was a real distinction between the two, though both plundered the Spanish treasure fleets. Privateers were patriots. They fitted out ships at their own expense and sailed forth, with their sovereigns' blessing, to plunder the ships of their countries' enemies. Privateers were considered respectable. They carried letters of marque from their sovereign and shared their spoils with the Crown. The pirates were men without a country, who attacked ships of all nations. Sometimes privateers turned pirates.

The French corsairs under Francis I of France were the first privateers to attack the Spanish galleons. One famed corsair, Jean Florin, is said to have confessed that he had robbed and sunk 150 Spanish ships before he was captured and beheaded by the Spanish. French corsairs sacked Havana in 1555, held the wealthy for ransom, and left the town with vast spoils three weeks later. Captain François le Clerc, "Peg-leg," led this expedition. Montbars the Exterminator was another of the famous French corsairs.

Queen Elizabeth encouraged the first English privateers when she came to the throne in 1558. Sir John Hawkins, slave smuggler and privateer, was knighted by the queen for his prowess against the cities of the Spanish Main. Francis Drake, who was to become one of England's most lustrous heroes, was the captain of a small ship in Hawkins's fleet. When the Spanish fleet sank four of Hawkins's ships and he lost all his treasure, Sir John ended his expeditions. Drake conducted a one-man war against Spain in the New World henceforth.

Drake, who never regarded himself or was regarded, even by his enemies, as a pirate, made one of his greatest exploits when he sailed around the world between 1577 and 1580, attacking Spaniards as he went. In 1585 he led a full-scale naval operation with more than twenty ships against the Spanish colonies in the West Indies. He conquered Santo Domingo, Havana, Cartagena, and Panama and destroyed the fort that the Spaniards were building at St. Augustine in Florida. Knighted, Sir Francis Drake went on to become Admiral Drake and to defeat the Spanish Armada and save England. He left his bones in the New World when he died on another expedition in 1595 off the coast of the Isthmus of Panama.

The terms "freebooter," "flibustier," and "buccaneer" were other names for the pirates of the Caribbean. The word "boucan" means the process of curing strips of meat by smoking over a slow fire, and "buccaneer" was first used to describe the men who were doing this in the Greater Antilles. On these larger islands both cattle and pigs had gone wild from the vast ranches, and men who were looking for a wild, free life made their living by hunting and by selling hides and smoked meat to passing ships. They soon turned to piracy. Most of the desperadoes in these outlaw bands were English or French, and they congregated on the eastern end of Hispaniola. They came to be a loosely knit confraternity with conventions and customs of their own, and called themselves the "Brotherhood of the Coast."

Buccaneers included shipwrecked sailors, deserters from ships, runaway indentured servants, criminals, and a few daring spirits who simply thirsted for adventure. They wore peaked caps and stained pantaloons and were armed with firelocks and belts full of knives. Pirates in small boats counted on surprise and terror to enable them to take the larger ships they captured. They would swarm over the sides of the galleons in the dusk and slaughter the officers before these knew what was happening. Each man in the pirate crew, including the cabin boy, was allotted a share of the booty according to articles he signed at the beginning of the voyage. Rewards were given for sighting a prize. A pirate who lost an eye in battle received an extra hundred pieces of eight.

Tortuga, an island just north of Hispaniola, was settled first by Huguenots as a French outpost in 1635. They found that it was an international haunt of buccaneers. The Huguenot leader, Le Vasseur, fortified Tortuga and became the robber leader in this notorious pirate stronghold. The island was captured by the Spanish, and the buccaneers retreated to the forests of northern Hispaniola, but they returned when the Spanish withdrew.

English buccaneers, outnumbered by the French, left for Jamaica. There they headquartered at Port Royal, initially with the tacit approval of Jamaica's governor. They were enlisted in 1665, through an English grant of "reprisal" or pardon, as mercenaries to fight Spain and were paid by the plunder they seized. The famous pirate Henry Morgan reigned over the villains at Port Royal during this period, and he was knighted for his service against Spanish forces. He excelled in surprise attacks and was infamous for his torture of prisoners. Boldly he sacked the Spanish Main. After some ten years of plundering, he was made lieutenant-governor of Jamaica, and died in 1688 still possessed of his loot. Wicked Port Royal perished, punished for its sins, said the pious, when it was swallowed by the sea in an earthquake in 1692.

None of the pirates were more famous than Captain William Kidd. He started his career as a privateer and had a fine home and a wife in New York, where he was respected as an honest ship's captain. He was sent by England to quell pirates in the Indian ocean, where he turned pirate himself. After swarming over the bulwarks of rich East Indiamen and Spanish galleons in the Caribbean, he was finally captured and hanged in London in 1701.

Blackbeard, a huge and ferocious man, was one of the most bloodthirsty of the pirates who haunted the Caribbean. Born Edward Teach, he got his nickname from the great black beard that reached nearly to his waist. St. Thomas in the Virgin Islands was one of his favorite harbors. Then he moved on to New Providence Island in the Bahamas as his headquarters. Thence he sailed to plunder the coast of the Carolinas, where he seems to have had some sort of agreement with Governor Charles Eden of North Carolina. The Carolinians appealed to

Governor Alexander Spotswood of Virginia, who sent an expedition down Pamlico Sound to get Blackbeard, dead or alive. The pirate was surprised off Ocracoke and there, after fierce hand-to-hand fighting between the courageous Lieutenant Robert Maynard of the Royal Navy and Blackbeard, the bay ran red with the blood of Edward Teach. Maynard took his head on a pike back to Virginia to prove he was dead.

Among the long list of notorious pirates were two women, Mary Read and Anne Bonny. Both sailed with Calico Jack Rackham. Mary fought a duel with a bullying pirate to save a young man whom the pirates had captured and with whom she had fallen in love. She killed the bully and married her sweetheart, but she was captured and sentenced to be hanged in the Bahamas. She died suddenly in prison. The old stories say that though Anne Bonny was captured, she was never hanged.

The French brothers Jean and Pierre Lafitte of New Orleans have a special niche in history. They plundered craft in the Gulf of Mexico, raided slavers, and became rich. But they called out their pirate crews to fight with General Andrew Jackson against the British and help the United States forces win the Battle of New Orleans during the War of 1812. After that they sailed off to loot again and were based on the Texas coast near what is now Galveston. Their end is not known.

Another of these latter-day pirates was the Spaniard José Gaspar, known as Gasparilla, who was based on the Gulf coast of Florida. When about to be captured by a United States warship in 1822, he wrapped a heavy anchor chain around his waist, jumped from his ship, and drowned.

For three hundred years piracy flourished in the Caribbean, and it took the United States Navy, under the command of Commodore David Porter, to sweep the buccaneers from that sea. In the 1820s the desperadoes had become so harrowing that the United States Congress appropriated $500,000 to outfit a squadron to rid the world of the sea raiders. England cooperated. For two years Commodore Porter's fleet swept the seas, capturing scores of pirate ships and making the pirates prisoners. In their pursuit, young Lieutenant, later Admiral, David Farragut, distinguished himself. Among the worst of those who were captured was the cruel Coferece, who, like many pirates, turned coward in the end and was garroted. By 1830, robbers who sailed under the Jolly Roger, the black flag with the skull and crossbones upon it, had disappeared completely from the waters of the New World.

They live on in song and story, and tales of buried treasure.

CLIMATE

The Caribbean islands enjoy what is called a tropical marine climate, as fine as any in the world. Under the benign sun, the average temperature ranges, from coldest to warmest months, between seventy-five and eighty-five degrees. The silken trade winds blowing across the Atlantic air-condition the land. Frost is almost unknown from the Bahamas to the Guianas. Only the highest mountains of the Greater Antilles are occasionally touched with frost. Night temperatures are usually pleasantly cool, no matter how warm the days. They sometimes fall to fifty-five degrees in the lowlands.

The wind patterns of the Caribbean determine the climate to a large extent. The control for these patterns is a high-pressure area known to weathermen as the "Azores-Bermuda high," because it lies between those two island groups. Around this high, winds flow in a clockwise direction, because of the earth's rotation. Near Africa they are northerly winds, near the Equator easterly, but over most of the ocean between Europe and the Caribbean they are northeasterly and hence are known as the northeasterly trade winds. In the South Atlantic a similar wind pattern produces the southeasterly trades.

In between lie the calm doldrums, where ascending columns of warm air condense to form huge rain-laden clouds. The shift of the Azores-Bermuda high, plus the humidity of the winds, determines both rainfall and hurricanes. The seasons are thought of as "wet and dry" rather than as "summer and winter." The equatorial rain belt moves north in the summer and south in the winter, and the islands get their rain when it is overhead.

The rain of the Caribbean seems wetter than rain in temperate zones, and it falls in big, fat, warm drops. Showers are usually brief and heavy. The eastern slopes of the mountainous large islands usually get the most rainfall, because the trade winds must rise over them and are condensed into showers. On some small, low islands, such as Aruba in the Netherlands Antilles, it rarely rains at all. Aruba, however, is out of all hurricane tracks and has natural air-conditioning in the steady trade winds. The Arubans distill drinking water from the sea and consider their climate perfect. Other less advanced islands that must depend on rainfall for their water may suffer periodically from drought.

In the Greater Antilles the islands are large enough to have a regular cycle of rain during the wet season. Land cools more rapidly than the surrounding ocean at night, and warms more rapidly in the day. The warm air rises from the land during the morning and condenses above an island as puffy white cumulus clouds. These spread, get bigger, denser, darker. They fall in heavy, brief showers in midafternoon, often accompanied by fine displays of thunder and lightning. By late afternoon the skies are blue again and the nights are cool and clean.

From June to November, troughs of low pressure called "easterly waves" often form in the doldrums north of the Equator. They bring rain to both the Lesser and Greater Antilles as they move west. Sometimes these waves begin to circulate around a low-pressure center in a counterclockwise direction, and a hurricane is born. As you face the hurricane winds, the center of the storm is on your right. Hurricane winds may reach two hundred miles an hour. The whole hurricane moves west or northwest through the island very slowly, usually at about ten miles an hour. The center of the storm is calm and windless, with blue skies above. Do not go out in it, for winds on the other side of the center will be howling again in a few minutes.

It is possible and practical to build houses and other buildings that will withstand all hurricanes, as South Florida has proved and as some of the Caribbean islands are learning. However, the real threat lies in the unpredictable storm wave that accompanies some hurricanes. The wave depends on the angle of approach of the wind to the shore, the slope of the ocean floor, the curve of the coast, and the height of the tide. The storm wave is the killer, rather than the big wind, when coastal stretches are suddenly flooded.

Connoisseurs of hurricane sunsets say the skies that precede these great storms are so beautiful that they are worth the big winds that follow. Nobody in the Caribbean says anything good about the northers that occasionally blow out of the cold heart of North America in winter to chill Cuba and Jamaica. These raw winds last only a few days. Warmed as they travel over the warm ocean, they never chill the southern Caribbean islands.

The climate of the tropics was once considered unhealthy, because it is healthy for disease-carrying mosquitoes and rodents. With the control of malaria, yellow fever, typhus, and cholera, these islands have come to be considered splendid health resorts. Since the unkind winter wind of the North and its attendant evils are still uncontrolled, the trek of sun seekers mounts annually. This great migration south is a twentieth-century phenomenon that can be attributed to the control of the so-called tropical diseases.

As for the notion that the lovely climate makes people indolent, this is not borne out by the few studies that have been made on climatic optimums. These studies indicate that a person can change his feeling about what is best in climate temperatures in a very few years. One such study showed that a person from Maine who considers a temperature of seventy-two degrees ideally warm and eighty-two degrees enervatingly hot, may require only about three years to accustom himself to enjoying strenuous work and play in eighty-two-degree weather.

GEOLOGY

The geological story of the Caribbean is a story of periods of upthrusting mountains and volcanoes that were then planed down in warm periods by the rising sea. The oldest rocks in the West Indies are those that were formed about the time when the first reptiles and insects appeared on earth, in the late Paleozoic era.

The dominant features of the area are the mountain chains that extend from the continental mainland eastward to form the islands. One of these mountain ranges made southern Cuba, Hispaniola, Puerto Rico, and the Virgin Islands. Another formed Jamaica. This happened in a period of great folding and wrinkling of the earth's crust about seventy million years ago, at the end of the Cretaceous period. Then the quivering earth quieted, the seas rose, and many of the volcanoes on the islands were buried under thick layers of limestone formed in the sea.

Later, about twenty-five million years ago, the earth again went through a period of making mountains and volcanoes, and the inner volcanic chain of the Lesser Antilles was formed. Trinidad's oil and Jamaica's bauxite were also formed at about the same time, in the Cenozoic era. Today three volcanoes are occasionally active in the Lesser Antilles — on Guadeloupe, St. Vincent, and Martinique. Boiling sulphur springs called *sou-frières*, found on numerous islands, indicate dying volcanoes. A fault that stretches through the Caribbean has caused many earthquakes. The pirate stronghold of Port Royal on Jamaica sank beneath the sea in an earthquake in 1692, and that island has had several earth shocks since then. The Windward Islands, Guadeloupe, the Virgin Islands, Port-au-Prince, and Cap-Haïtien have all had earthquakes from time to time.

Few mountains in the West Indies are today more than 7,000 feet high, though the Dominican Republic does have one 10,000-foot peak. The best evidence of the ancient earth folding in the region is found in the deep undersea troughs that separate the islands from the mainland and from each other. The Brownson Trough, one of the deepest parts of the Atlantic ocean, plunges to 30,000 feet in depth north of Puerto Rico. The Bartlett Trough is 20,000 feet deep and 1,000 miles long, extending from the coast of Honduras northeast-ward and passing between Cuba and Jamaica. The Anegada Trough, separating the Lesser Antilles from the Virgin Islands, is the only deep-water channel from the Atlantic into the Caribbean.

The principal agents now at work creating land in the Caribbean are the corals of the sea and the mangrove trees along the shore. Fringing reefs, barrier reefs, bank reefs, and atolls have been built by corals into land since the last Ice Age. Sand is deposited on these reefs by waves and wind, and they protect the shores from erosion. They also form exotically beautiful, fish-filled undersea gardens beloved by SCUBA divers and other explorers of the warm sea. Mangrove seeds are viable in salt water and can root themselves in mud covered by the sea at high tide. These land builders, which are found in the tropics and subtropics all around the world, seem to be walking to sea on their many roots, which trap sand and silt to extend the land.

VEGETATION IN THE CARIBBEAN

The green mantle that covers much of the Caribbean islands is most varied. The land-building mangroves grow in both brackish and salt water. Coconut palms, which thrive along the beaches, are usually planted by people. Casuarina trees, introduced from Australia in this century, fringe many shores. Their seeds are viable in salt water and by now have floated all around the Caribbean. These lacy evergreens, soughing in the trade winds, are a memorable keynote of the islands. On some of the islands that were heavily timbered in past centuries, cacti flourish and create a landscape like that of Arizona. High, handsome tropical rain forests, with myriad different trees, can still be enjoyed on some islands of the Lesser Antilles and on Trinidad. Orchids thrive in these glades. Resinous Caribbean pines stand tall on the slopes of hills and mountains. They are valued as hard-hearted timber. The rich vegetation differs from island to island. The volcanic slopes are far more fertile than the limestone.

Much of the land in the West Indies was cleared for planting in past centuries, and few virgin stands of woodland remain. On some islands, not only the character of the vegetation but the climate has been changed by cutting off the woodland cover. Some of the present forest cover is protected by law to prevent continuing erosion. Like almost all soils in warm climates, the land in these islands rather quickly loses its fertility through farming, erosion and oxidation. Minerals and organic materials are leached out and washed away in the heavy rains. The lowlands remain more fertile and are better managed. Slowly, modern agricultural methods, including the use of chemical fertilizers and giant machinery, are being introduced in a few of the islands.

The agricultural products of the islands have shaped life there. Tobacco was the New World's dubious gift to the Old and was one of the first crops of any importance in the region. The harvesting and curing of tobacco takes individual care. It does best on small farms, under the handling of skillful fingers. In colonial days Virginia raised better tobacco than did the West Indies. In the 1640s the islanders learned how to squeeze sugar cane to produce sugar, and the islands' fate was sealed. Production of sugar cane requires many, many acres, and slaves or very cheap labor. It is still largely cut by hand. Profits from sugar production entrenched slavery in the Caribbean lands.

After Napoleon encouraged the raising of sugar beets, beginning in 1804, profits from the cane sugar of the tropics declined. But many acres on many islands are still given over to raising sugar cane. Today, more and more winter vegetables are being raised, and some are exported. But harvesting these crops breeds a low standard of living, too, and this is one of the saddest unsolved problems of this salad-loving century.

All sorts of fine fruit trees flourish, some native to the islands and some imported. They include avocados, mangoes, citrus, bananas, and coffee. The flowering trees, such as the magnificent royal poinciana, are among the chief delights of the islands.

SETTLEMENT OF THE CARIBBEAN ISLANDS

The Carib Indians who gave this part of the world its name have almost all gone, and the Arawak Indians have disappeared. In 1960 the census in the British West Indies listed only 1,810 people descended from Indians, all Carib. Aruba, in the Netherlands Antilles, boasts that on that island the native Indians were never exterminated. Indian blood can be marked in the lank black hair, the high cheekbones, and the friendly poise of these prideful people. The Dutch and Indian temperaments have made a most happy marriage on this island.

The Caribbean islands come in four flavors: Spanish, English, Dutch, and French. Those were the European nationalities that sent the first colonists. Columbus's colonists began to build the first outpost of Spain, Santo Domingo, on the island of Hispaniola in 1496. Today the city still thrives, and the island is divided between Haiti and the Dominican Republic. Jamaica was first settled in 1509 by Spaniards but was never considered of much importance by Spain. Cuba was colonized in 1511, with Santiago the first settlement. Havana later became more important. Spaniards under Juan Ponce de León began settlement of Puerto Rico in 1512.

After several failures, the English got their first permanent foothold in the Caribbean on St. Christopher (St. Kitts) in the Leeward Islands in 1622, and shortly thereafter they colonized Barbados, the Virgin Islands, Nevis, Antigua, Montserrat, and St. Lucia. Jamaica was captured by the British from the Spanish in a formal naval and military attack in 1655, when the Spanish population numbered only about 1,500. English colonists arrived in 1664.

Between 1630 and 1640 the Dutch, aggressively hostile to Spain, seized Curaçao, Saba, St. Martin, St. Eustatius, and Aruba, and Curaçao became the center of Dutch power in the West Indies. The French followed shortly, to settle Martinique and Guadeloupe in 1635. They later took Saint-Domingue, which is now Haiti, from the Spanish.

The white settlers were soon outnumbered by Negroes. The Negroes had many origins in Africa. They were described in old West Indian accounts as Senegalese, Coromantees, Whydahs, Nagoes, Pawpaws, Eboes, Mocoes, Congoes, Angolas, and Mandingoes. A fighting people, they first mutinied in Barbados in 1649. Maroons were once an important element on some islands. The word is derived from the Spanish *cimaroon* and means wild, escaped, free. It was applied to free Negroes, who sometimes in the sixteenth and seventeenth centuries lived with Indians, sometimes became pirates, and often lived in their own villages.

When the slaves were emancipated in the British West Indies in 1834, they numbered about 700,000, and they outnumbered white people by about seven to one. Their freedom left a vacuum—a need for laborers—and about half a million East Indians came to this part of the world between 1840 and 1920 as indentured laborers. Today descendants of these immigrants from Asia are found throughout the Caribbean.

On Cuba, by far the largest of the islands, the population was comparatively small until well along in the nineteenth century. Determined efforts in that century, plus accelerated development, attracted many new white immigrants. Under Spanish influence, Havana became what many United States visitors in the first half of this century remember as the most beautiful city in the Western World. At the time of Castro's advent, about thirty percent of the population was white. This percentage is second only to that found in Puerto Rico.

The African cultural heritage is strong in the islands today, predominantly black as they are. For some generations, where white people were driven out or retreated, mulattoes reigned socially and politically. In recent decades, pleasure and pride in being black has grown, and men of straight African descent are coming more and more to places of power and prestige.

There are many African survivals in the Caribbean. The maroons in the town of Accompong in Jamaica are descendants of the only maroons with whom England made a treaty, and the town is governed by maroon law and culture. In Jamaica, duppies (ghosts) are feared. In Antigua it is the jumbies (also ghosts) who must be placated. A mixture of African Obeah and Christianity is the religion in the back country.

Obeah conjurers, however, are not prone to poison their customers' enemies for pay with the numerous poison plants of the islands, as they did a century ago.

In the black republic of Haiti, since the Negroes freed themselves with a savage lunge in 1804 they have a sort of elected monarchy. There they also have voodoo, which is "the old mysticism of the world in African terms"—a religion of creation and life, a worship of the sun, the water, and other natural forces. The Haitian gods, mysteres, or loas are little affected by the Catholic saints with whom they consort in that world. Voodoo is as benign as most religions, but in Haiti it is whispered that there are also zombies and the Sect Rouge or Cochon Gris (gray pig). This is said to be a very secret society, detested by voodoo, forbidden by law, having nothing to do with the old voodoo religion.

Black people in the Caribbean today are working to drive out the ancient Bad, preserve the ancient Good. These descendants of slaves have inherited by their numbers some of the most beautiful islands in the world, and they have inherited them because of the same strength and hardihood that caused their ancestors to be brought to the islands. They are teaching song and dance and learning the arts of written eloquence and political organization. Few believe today, as slaves used to do, that when they die they will go back to Africa.

JAMAICA

In a Nutshell:

Large island with magnificent scenery, beautiful mountains, beaches, and resort towns. Size – 4,412 square miles. Well-developed tourist services, fine roads, excellent hotel accommodations. Golf, polo, horse racing, river rafting, sailing, tennis, game fishing, water skiing, night clubs. Capital is Kingston. Direct airline connections with North, Central, and South America, Europe, and other Caribbean Islands. Language: English. – Population: 1,900,000.

The original Arawak Indian settlers called it "Xaymaca"–a "land of wood and rivers"–and, in fact, more than a hundred rivers and streams flow through the island's mountainous terrain. Peaks soar to heights of more than 6,000 feet, and one, Blue Mountain Peak, is 7,402 feet high. Thus, Jamaica, an island of 4,412 square miles and the third largest of the Antilles, is something of a "continent in microcosm," containing all the geographical variations of undulating hills, mountains, plains, valleys, and seashore, as well as the climatic differences ranging from tropical beaches to chilly "hill stations." It has actually been known to snow on the very highest mountains.

Jamaica was discovered by Columbus, the very first Caribbean tourist, and was held by Spain until 1655. The gentle Arawaks were almost completely exter-

20

minated by the Spanish and were replaced by slaves from Africa.

Jamaica remained a colony of Spain for about 150 years. Then, in May 1655, a body of English sailors and soldiers landed in Kingston Harbour and marched on Spanish Town. The force was under Admiral Penn and General Venables, who had sailed to the West Indies on an expedition ordered by Oliver Cromwell, then the Lord Protector of England.

Taken by surprise, the Spaniards surrendered on the following day, and Jamaica fell into British hands. But the Spanish did not leave Jamaica without a struggle. Many of them took to the mountains and waged long guerilla warfare with the British. Not until 1660 did the last Spaniard, Don Arnaldo de Ysassi, flee the island.

With the departure of Ysassi (from the spot now known romantically as Runaway Bay, on the north coast), Jamaica became a British possession in fact. The first British governor, General D'Oyley, was appointed, and the long association of Jamaica with Great Britain began.

At about this time, the buccaneers, those bandits of the sea, made Port Royal their headquarters and made it, in turn, "the wealthiest and wickedest city on the face of the earth."

But the days of buccaneers were soon numbered. Their own leader, Henry Morgan, turned against them when he was knighted by the British sovereign and appointed lieutenant-governor of Jamaica. He outlawed his former freebooting colleagues, and hanged many of them at Port Royal.

Then Nature herself took final action to wipe out the pirates. On June 7, 1692, Port Royal was destroyed by earthquake. The wicked city, with all its wealth, slid under the sea beneath Kingston Harbour and signaled the end of the era of the Black Flag.

Sugar became the mainstay and principal source of the Jamaican economy in the eighteenth century. Almost a million African slaves passed through the flesh markets of Jamaica before slavery was abolished in 1833. Palatial estate houses still exist, many converted into hotels now, witnesses of the great days of old. And although sugar is still big business, tourism and an industrial boom fostered by United States and Canadian capital are assuming a new importance in the island's economy.

Jamaica has five Tourist Centers: Kingston, Montego Bay, Ocho Rios, Port Antonio, and Mandeville, and these attract tourists in such numbers that only Bermuda, Nassau, and Puerto Rico can stand as potential rivals. None of them has the spectacular scenery found here.

Kingston, capital city of Jamaica, surrounds a port that is the seventh largest in the world. Its main shopping street is King Street, a typical Caribbean Main Street, with shops, crowds, hawkers and much traffic – as colorful a thoroughfare as you are likely to find south of Miami. The Victoria Crafts Market is certainly one of the sights to see here, as well as the interesting and once mighty Fort Charles, a historical British stronghold. Visit Port Royal, once the bawdiest city in the New World, but now, what remains of it, a sleepy fishing village. Old-timers will tell you that the bells of sunken Christ Church still toll fathoms deep. In any case the hardy skin diver can see the ruins of old houses and forts still standing on the ocean floor in this ghostly underwater city. Landlubbers, however, will find all the facts and figures about Port Royal as well as other historic data about Jamaica contained in the Institute of Jamaica back in Kingston, which houses a museum, a natural history section, and an art gallery. One of Kingston's widely visited sites is actually five miles out of town. This is Hope Botanical Gardens, where you will find 200 acres of beautifully landscaped tropical trees, plants and flowers. More of the same are discoverable at Castleton Gardens, 19 miles from, and 2,000 feet above, Kingston. Here you are well above the heat and bustle of the capital and well on the road to the northern Jamaica coast resorts of Port Antonio, Ocho Rios, and Montego Bay. An afternoon at Kingston's famous Caymanas Race Track is well spent, and there are excellent golf courses on which to practice your game.

Montego Bay offers bathing at the world-renowned Doctor's Cave beach, one of the world's finest, with its translucent water and white sand floor. Outside the hotel area, the island carries on its own way of life, mostly in agricultural pursuits. The parish of St. James, of which Montego Bay is the principal town, is one of the largest producers of sugar and bananas in Jamaica.

Ocho Rios is in perhaps one of the oldest areas of the island. This part of the north coast is redolent with memories of Columbus and the early days of the Spanish occupation. Here are Discovery Bay and Runaway Bay; here are the sites of Santa Gloria and Sevilla Nueva. Ruined walls and ancient buildings are vivid evidence of the antiquity of the area.

There are also Fern Gully and Dunn's River Falls, two scenic beauty spots. The former is a tropical gorge filled with profusion of ferns, into which the sun penetrates only dimly, to create an otherworldly effect. The Falls are the most spectacular in the island, cascading down a natural rock stairway onto a white sand beach.

At Port Antonio, the main attraction is rafting on the Rio Grande, one of the island's largest rivers. This is a water sport unique to the island. Another attractive spot is the Blue Lagoon, which has been developed as a recreational center. Noted for its fishing, Port Antonio is the home of the Jamaica International Fishing Tournament, held in the fall of each year.

Leaving the coast towns, we plunge into the fantastic interior of Jamaica. Here is one of the most primitive, wild, and violent areas in all the West Indies, called the Cockpit Country, where descendants of fugitive slaves, known as maroons, still exist, although they are now peaceful, hard-working farmers. Continuing inland, we will arrive at Mandeville, the cool summer capital of Jamaica. Here is a corner of a foreign field that is forever England, for the rolling hills and quaint country churches remind one of many an English shire. The village green, the Georgian courthouse, the neat cottages and gardens are all remembrances of the mother country.

Mandeville is Jamaica's mountain country. Situated 2,000 feet above sea level, it has a bracing climate and the pace is leisurely. Because of its air of quiet repose, Mandeville has come to be known as Jamaica's "English village," complete with village green and parish church. It has its own beauty spot in nearby Bamboo Grove and an excellent golf course.

Jamaica has a rich cultural life. Artistic feeling finds expression in many ways. The work of the country's outstanding painters is to be seen on display throughout the island, capturing the warmth and glow, the color and the beauty, the happiness and humor of Jamaican life. There are many art galleries.

Music plays a great part in Jamaican life. Regular concerts and recitals keep public taste stimulated, and there are orchestras, choirs, and individual musicians who make a contribution to musical activity. The Jamaica Military Band, a colorful group, is a national institution.

Folk songs and folk music give vivid insight into the character and outlook of the people. Jamaican folk songs may be described as Africanized versions of English ballads, given a distinctly indigenous nature by vivid imagery, wit, humor, irony, and satire. There is no great poetry, but this is more than compensated for by the color and rhythm of the music.

Just as they are natural musicians, Jamaicans are gifted and talented dancers, with an imaginative sense of rhythm and movement. Dancing forms another facet of Jamaican artistic life. Traditional classical ballet is performed, and Jamaican music and legend are used to conceive modern dance creations. There are organized groups who give regular recitals.

Bringing a touch of carnival to the Christmas holiday season is John Canoe, a traditional Christmas mummery that goes back to the days of slavery. John Canoe, the central figure, was a ceremonial performer in the old Gold Coast. The slaves transported him to Jamaica and surrounded him with English-style Pantomime figures such as they saw in the Great Houses of their masters. Then, to the primitive music of goatskin drum and bamboo fife, these bands of masked and costumed dancers performed for the lords and ladies of the sugar estates. Today, the tradition is carried on in rural Jamaica, and John Canoe shows form part of the entertainment fare in some resort hotels.

Such are only the highlights of the sights that any tourist to Jamaica will welcome. It is a land of happy living – as any visitor will tell you. The music of calypso melodies seems to be everywhere, and there is a gaiety in the air that keeps attracting repeat vacationers every year. Jamaica has been since 1962 an independent country and a full-fledged member of the British Commonwealth.

HAITI

In a Nutshell:

Most exotic country in the Caribbean. Beautiful mountain scenery, great historic monuments. The people, religion, culture, folklore, and art are unique and outstanding. Free port facilities. Size – 10,714 square miles. Population: 4,660,000. Excellent hotel accommodations, particularly in Port-au-Prince, Pétionville, and Cap-Haïtien. Capital City: Port-au-Prince. Good airline connections with North and South America and the other Caribbean Islands. Golf, tennis, hunting, fishing, art exhibits, cockfights, nightclubbing, and gambling casino. Languages: French and English.

Haitians are descended from people who came from Senegal, the Sudan, the African Gold Coast, the Congo – and from France. The folk patterns of half the tribes of Africa have found their way to Haiti along with the cultural background of Europe's most civilized country. And so the stage is set for presenting a land of vivid

contrasts of the old and new, the African and French, the Christian and pagan, the sophisticated and primitive. Modern air-conditioned villas, gingerbread mansions, luxury hotels, and native huts are all part of the scene. Burros and Cadillacs mingle on the streets of Port-au-Prince, Haiti's capital. Here you will find the sophisticated wit of a Parisian salon and the fascinating beat of a voodoo drum.

Haiti occupies the western third of the island of Hispaniola (as it was called), which it shares with the Dominican Republic. It was "Hayti" (The Mountain Country) to the aboriginal Arawaks. It is related that the Spanish colonists "fell upon their knees and then fell upon the natives" in their search for gold. Having exterminated the Indians, the Spanish imported the proudest tribes of Africa to work their plantations and build their cities. It was their descendants who would sound the tocsin of revolution, probably the bloodiest known in the Americas, in answer to the Haitian's unquenchable spirit of independence. Such colorful figures as Toussaint L'Ouverture, Jean Jacques Dessalines, and King Henri Christophe soon took the stage in the Haitian Wars of Independence.

Shaped like the open mouth of a giant sea monster,

Haiti is more vertical than horizontal. Blue-green mountains rise up on either side with occasional white-walled villages dotting the coastline. And parts of Haiti are still as unexplored and remote as Brazil's Matto Grosso.

The happy capital of this amazing country is Port-au-Prince. An endless procession of peasants and townfolk, afoot or on donkey, mingle with Buicks and Cadillacs, taxis and busses blaring their way through the narrow streets of the Old City and the wider boulevards of the newer sections of town. Shops are contained in massive colonial buildings, and the visitor can purchase anything from rare imported perfumes to Haitian rum, from American milk of magnesia to the finest English china. Best of all is the limitless variety of polished mahogany, most beautiful of all Haitian woods.

The National Museum contains interesting exhibits and relics of Haiti's exciting history, including the anchor of Columbus's flagship, the *Santa Maria*. A variety of old churches, some dating back to 1720, add picturesqueness to the city. The Episcopal Cathedral of the Holy Trinity contains the celebrated murals, which are the most important single monument of Haitian primitive art. No visitor should miss the Iron Market, a combination of the Caledonia Market, the Marché aux Puces in Paris, and an Oriental bazaar. In the more recently developed part of the city, you will discover buildings of more modern design: shops, government and airline offices, consulates, embassies, and theaters. Charming sidewalk cafés in the French manner are everywhere.

Overlooking Port-au-Prince are the mountain resort villages of Pétionville (2,000 feet), Kenscoff (6,000 feet), and Furcy (7,000 feet). At Kenscoff, the native market is an unforgettable sight. Furcy provides an awe-inspiring view of Port-au-Prince and the surrounding countryside. From here one can see Haiti's highest mountain peak, La Selle, almost 9,000 feet above sea level.

In Port-au-Prince and up to Pétionville and Kenscoff, some of the world's most beautiful resort hotels have been developed in the interest of attracting tourists. Most of these hostelries offer what no man could create – an assortment of magnificent panoramic views of the Haitian countryside.

Cap-Haïtien, or Le Cap as it is called, is a city of indescribable Creole charm. Although it is the second city of the republic in size, it is really first in historic interest and picturesque beauty. A short trip from Le Cap will lead you to the formidable fortress of La Citadelle, built by Henri Christophe. This has been called the eighth wonder of the world: the walls are 140 feet high and 12 feet thick at the base. It is built on the top of a mountain whose only approach is by horse or mule and guide. The battlements and terraced stonework are reminiscent of the Middle Ages. Some 200,000 ex-slaves were conscripted for the work, and 20,000 died during the construction of the Citadelle. More than a masterpiece of architectural engineering, the Citadelle stands as a fantastic symbol of man's will.

More charming are the ruins of the royal palace of Sans Souci, which Henri Christophe intended to be a kind of "New World Versailles." With the aid of one's imagination, one can almost visualize Sans Souci as it appeared early in the nineteenth century: spacious galleries and rooms paneled with mahogany and draped in Gobelin tapestries, gilded mirrors and fine paintings. Courtiers and royal family dressed to the teeth in satins and brocades, bizarre copies of the pomp of Europe. The palace had 365 doors, one for every day of the year, and the first nonelectric air-conditioning system in the Americas.

Haiti the exotic, Haiti the bizarre has nothing more truly fascinating than the living practice of Voodoo. Voodooism is a barbaric African religion which flourishes in Haiti in spite of official condemnation by the Catholic Church. Answering some deep, primitive need in the Haitian soul, it is a vital religious practice, complete with its own ritual.

No story of Haiti is complete without a word about Haitian painting and folk art. The churches, hotels, airport, shops, and Exhibition Buildings are aglow with murals painted by self-taught primitive local artists. Haitian paintings are sold all over the world and have their place in the foremost galleries and art museums of the world.

The Haitian you will meet is by nature a good-tempered, affable, and friendly person. The white tourist will never encounter any sign of hostility. The wealthier classes are really interested in politics, literature, and art, and many have the advantage of a superior French academic education. They are, in general, as polished, polite, worldly, sophisticated, and suave as any Parisian.

Even among the poorer folk, there is a kind of buoyancy, a *joie de vivre*, a zest for carefree living that adds immeasurably to the charm of the country.

24

DOMINICAN REPUBLIC
The Land that Columbus Loved Best

In a Nutshell:

Rich country with high mountains, well-developed agriculturally, good roads, and oldest colonial historical monuments in the Western Hemisphere. Columbus is buried here. Size – 19,129 square miles. Capital: Santo Domingo. Excellent hotel accommodations. Night clubs, gambling casino, golf, polo, tennis, fishing, boating. Airline connections with North and South America and the other Caribbean Islands. Languages: Spanish and English. Population: 3,550,000.

Haiti's sister republic on historic Hispaniola is the Dominican Republic, which occupies the eastern two-thirds of the island. After Cuba, it is the second largest of the Greater Antilles. A land of green and fruitful valleys, it boasts four mountain ranges whose majesty and beauty – rising as they do from the blue Carribean to heights of more than 10,400 feet – have caused tourists to grow ecstatic.

Not the least of these nature-intoxicated tourists was Columbus, who discovered the island in 1492. The capital city of Santo Domingo was settled by Columbus's brother, Bartolomé, in 1496 and is therefore the oldest city in the New World. As such, the city has a number of "firsts" to its credit: the first church, the first school, the first mint, and the first city council. Also the first Negro slaves to be brought to the New World came through Santo Domingo. On Hispaniola, tobacco was first tasted by the white man, and a new and terrifying word found its way into European languages – "hurricane".

From its very promising and flourishing outset as a Spanish colony – such eminent travelers as Cortés, Pizarro, Ponce de León, and Balboa passed through its portals – Santo Domingo began to decline in importance as the gold of Mexico and Peru started to pour into the coffers of Spain. More than 300 years of misfortune followed. Sir Francis Drake sacked and plundered the capital; French buccaneers seized the part known as Haiti, hurricanes and political unrest were prevalent. The revolution of 1844 swept the Haitian troops of occupation from the country, and the Dominican Republic was established as a completely independent entity.

In recent years, there have been considerable achievements. Santo Domingo has been so modernized that many refer to it as the "Washington of the Tropics." Refugees from Europe have assisted in this development. The economy is quite stable.

Santo Domingo is a storehouse of history, and despite the damage done by Drake and the destruction of the violent 1930 hurricane, which almost leveled the city, there are enough relics of the sixteenth century to delight every visitor.

Among the many churches, the greatest is the Cathedral of Santa Maria la Menor, where some of the Admiral's bones lie buried in an elaborate marble sepulcher. This cathedral is a treasurehouse of colonial Spain, containing paintings by Murillo, silver by Cellini, and an emperor's ransom in jewels. All the sixteenth-century churches are well kept, as is that minor gem of colonial architecture, the fortress home of Diego Columbus, the admiral's son. Called the Alcázar, it was painstakingly restored and reconstructed and is one of the major tourist experiences in all the Caribbean.

While the Alcázar was being built, Diego Columbus resided in the House of the Cord (built in 1502), the oldest house still standing in the Western Hemisphere. Not far away is the Columbus Ceiba, a stump of the silk cotton tree to which Columbus tied his ship when it moored in the Ozama River. The National Museum contains fascinating pre-Columbian artifacts and grotesques made by the vanished Indians. All these are housed in what was formerly Diego's stables and servants' quarters.

Modern Santo Domingo is a truly gleaming capital city. It is bright with magnificent boulevards and has a permanent civic center, which was formerly the International Peace and Progress Fair Grounds of 1956, complete with mammoth outdoor theater, casino, and imposing public buildings. Many lovely parks grace the city, with one, in particular, for children. The adjacent botanical gardens are splendid, with caves containing pre-Columbian petroglyphs.

Other points of interest are the pink-marble National Palace, the impressive structures of University City, and, in preparation, the Columbus Memorial Lighthouse. The memorial is to be a gigantic recumbent cross, a half mile long and 120 feet high. It is an international project, approved by the United Nations. When completed, twenty-one avenues, one for each of the American Republics, will radiate from the head of the cross.

A superb modern highway takes you out of Santo Domingo to the popular resort of Boca Chica, where a lovely lagoon, more than a mile long, offers perfect swimming and other aquatic pleasures. Other countryside routes take you past flourishing fields and mountains covered with mahogany trees and plantations of cane, coffee, and cocoa.

Most European and American travelers are surprised and delighted with the country's cleanliness and, more particularly, with the cultivated appearance of Santo Domingo's beautiful boulevards and homes.

PUERTO RICO

In a Nutshell:

Highly developed by the United States. Interesting old cities. Fast-growing tourist center. Beautiful mountain scenery and fine beaches. Excellent roads. Size – 3423 square miles. Capital: San Juan, a large commercial metropolis with a well-kept historical quarter. Fishing (marlin, dolphin, kingfish, tuna, bonito, sailfish, tarpon), golf, tennis, water skiing, hunting, horseback riding, gambling casinos. Excellent hotel accommodations. Direct airline connections with North, South, and Central America, Europe, and the other Caribbean Islands. Languages: Spanish and English. Population: 2,800,000.

"Que puerto rico!" exclaimed Ponce de León when he first caught a glimpse of the island's main harbor in 1508. "What a fine harbor!" He was referring, of course, to the site of what is now the city of San Juan. Actually, the Spanish settlement erected on this locale was called Puerto Rico (1519). The island had earlier been named San Juan Bautista by Columbus in 1493. How and why the city subsequently got the name of the country, and vice versa, is not clear even among historians. It is believed, however, that some early colonial mapmaker exchanged the names in error.

After 400 years of Spanish occupation, Puerto Rico was ceded to the United States after the Spanish-American War in 1898, and its inhabitants have been American citizens since 1917. Since 1952, the island has been a self-governing commonwealth.

Once upon a time – and that was not very long ago – Puerto Rico was a totally foreign island, poor, blighted, unhappy, and overcrowded. It is still overcrowded (it is the densely populated home of 2,800,000 people), but "Operation Bootstrap" has made a successful economic assault on poverty and lack of industry. It was designed for Puerto Rico by Puerto Ricans. Prominently responsible for this ambitious program of social and economic progress was the popular governor Luis Muñoz Marín,

who was also the first governor freely elected in Puerto Rico. It was his idea that Puerto Rico, previously a much-neglected United States possession, had to advance through its own efforts. Special government agencies, a Planning Board (1942), the Water Resources Authority (for development of a power system), the Government Development Bank for financing and *Fomento,* and the Economic Development Administration for the promotion of the idea were set up. Today the island bristles in a kind of cultural and economic renaissance in which education, commerce, and tourism contribute equal shares toward brightening present and future social conditions.

Geologically speaking, Puerto Rico is the crest of a submarine mountain range rising from the sea bed about 32,200 feet (Cerro de Punta, the island's highest point, is only 4,398 feet above sea level). Its situation in the Caribbean could not be more fortunate, since it stands at the crossroads of the Greater and Lesser Antilles and on an air route between North and South America.

The old and the new meet in San Juan with startling impact. The International Airport at Isla Verde is one of the world's major modern terminals. In a matter of minutes, however, you are whisked by cab or by bus (called Guaguas) to Old San Juan. Despite the juxta-

position of old Spanish buildings and modern houses, the atmosphere of colonial Spain still permeates the Old Town. The sights of interest most frequented by visitors are the Morro Castle, one of the strongest of old Caribbean forts; the sixteenth-century Cathedral where Ponce de León is buried, San José Church, San Juan Gate, tiny Christo Chapel, and a beautiful old mansion built for Ponce's son-in-law 97 years before the Pilgrims arrived at Plymouth Rock. The governor's residence, called the Fortaleza, is in this part of the city, as well. One of the outstanding hotels is El Convento, right in the center of Old San Juan. Three hundred years ago it was a convent; today it is one of the reconstructed glories of Puerto Rico.

With more than four thousand miles of very good roads, Puerto Rico makes it easy for the visitor to see the national and historical marvels outside the capital.

For a half day's trip out of San Juan, visit El Yunque (The Anvil), a forty-five-minute drive from the city. This is the superb tropical rain forest – the Caribbean National Forest. El Yunque is actually the name of the mountain peak to which one ascends through a cool, exciting forest world with splashing mountain waterfalls. A restaurant and cabins are provided for those who wish to linger, ride horseback, or swim in the cold mountain pool.

On the return to San Juan, one may stop at Luquillo Beach, one of the most beautiful in the Caribbean. Fringed with palm trees, it is a sweeping half-moon of white sand and gently slopes to the waterline. Picnics here are a favorite pastime.

For a visit to Ponce and the south coast, a minimum of two or three days should be allowed if one is to absorb all the wonders to be seen.

Ponce, Puerto Rico's second city, is called the "Pearl of the South." Not quite so cramped as San Juan's Old City, Ponce allowed itself room to build spacious Spanish patios, garden balconies, and colonial mansions. It is considered by many to be more colorfully Spanish than San Juan.

Ponce has two lovely *plazuelas,* with the Cathedral of Our Lady of Guadalupe between them. Probably the most-often photographed subject in the city is the old Ponce firehouse (now a museum), the Parque de Bombas. It is painted in glaring red and black stripes and adorned with gray, yellow, and green ornaments.

Also in Ponce are the first Protestant church ever authorized in the Spanish dominions in America – a gift of Queen Victoria of England – and the new Ponce Intercontinental Hotel, a luxury hotel of spacious dimensions that has provided a powerful stimulus to the tourist trade in these parts. Here, too, is a monument to Puerto Rico's great musical composer, Juan Morel Campos. Among the latter's masterpieces are the "Juegos Florales," "The Symphony of Puerto Rico," and a number of exquisite piano pieces, often played by the island's leading pianist, Jesús María Sanroma.

Mayagüez is the third-largest city of Puerto Rico and an important port. It lies at the western tip of the island. The embroidery and needlework for which the island is famous stem largely from Mayagüez enterprises. A branch of the University of Puerto Rico – the College of Agriculture and Mechanical Arts – is here, as well as an agricultural experiment station conducted by the United States government and reputed to house the largest collection of tropical plants in the New World.

The coastal route passes through the fishing village and resort of La Parguera, where that singular marvel of nature – "The Bay of Living Light," or Phosphorescent Bay – is situated. The waters cast off a luminous glow at night that it is almost possible to read by. Heading north, the motorist will visit San Germán, an extremely ancient town founded by Diego Columbus, the son of the Discoverer. The Porta Coeli Church here (1513) is a relic of great interest.

Rural Puerto Rico is, to some, the most charming part of the island. Here one sees the cabins of the *jíbaros*, as the peasants are called, tucked away behind trees and shrubbery throughout the countryside.

Most of the luxury hotels offer tourists the excitement of government-sponsored gambling casinos.

In Puerto Rico, the sportsman is king. Facilities and conditions for almost every kind of fishing are ideal. Renowned for the deep-sea fishing off its coasts, the island offers shallow-water and even lake fishing. Blue and white marlin, tuna, sailfish, dolphin, wahoo, mackerel, barracuda, bonito, kingfish, tarpon, snook, snapper, and bonefish are among the hundreds of species found in Puerto Rican waters.

Another aquatic sport is water skiing, and if one spends any time on the island one will certainly take up skin diving. Every big hotel has tennis courts, and a few hold international tournaments.

Golf enthusiasts will need no reminder of the superb courses on this island. Most mountain resorts in Puerto Rico provide facilities for horseback riding.

The atmosphere of Puerto Rico – and particularly San Juan – is a bright and happy one. Its night life glitters with the entertainment of international stars; the casinos are busy taking money away from its guests in the most delightful ways; the restaurants provide some of the finest assortments of foods, prepared in the Continental, American, or Puerto Rican manner; the shops are filled with the merchandise of the world, and although modernism is the key word in the development of architecture, housing, industry, and tourism, much remains of the old-world charm that endears Puerto Rico to an ever-widening circle of Caribbean visitors.

THE VIRGIN ISLANDS

It is difficult to express one's first impressions on sighting the Virgin Islands in the distance across the unique blue of the Caribbean – a dark emerald necklace, crescent-shaped, of more than one hundred island jewels gleaming in the tropical sun. Closer, one notes the jagged peaks that rise starkly from the sea, coral reefs that boil with the foamy onslaught of ocean waves, palm-fringed beaches of white sand which are among the world's best, and winding channels of placid azure waters that separate the Virgins from one another. Even on closer approach, the islands look absolutely virginal, unspoiled, and uninhabited – silent sentinels, each within sight of each other, of Caribbean tranquillity.

It is only just before arrival that one begins to see signs of human habitation – the colorful, pastel-tinted buildings of Charlotte Amalie covering the hillsides of the city. Some 200,000 tourists visit the Virgin Islands annually to soak up the sun and imbibe the more refreshing and relaxing aspects of contemporary civilization in an area so lovely that "angels pause to rest here on their visits between earth and heaven."

The curious name of the islands is attributed to Columbus, who first sighted them on St. Ursula's Day in 1493 and made them a memorial to the virgins who were martyred with her in defense of their chastity. A historical ambiguity exists, inasmuch as two of the three principal United States islands are named for male saints – St. Thomas and St. John – and the third is called St. Croix – Holy Cross.

ST. THOMAS
(U. S. Virgin Islands)

In a Nutshell:

Tourist center of the Virgin Islands. Size: 32 square miles. A free port. Beautiful scenery, quaint restaurants, night clubs. Good hotel accommodations. Capital: Charlotte Amalie. Visit the excellent free-port shops here. Horse racing, golf, tennis, hunting, fishing, sailing. Excellent airline connections to the United States, Canada, Puerto Rico, and the other Caribbean Islands. Languages: English, Spanish, and Danish.

Among the many historical personalities of colonial days who came to know and love St. Thomas, second largest of the U. S. Virgin Islands, were bloodthirsty characters like Captain Kidd and Blackbeard the Pirate.

With such vivid and exciting figures on hand, one would expect the history of St. Thomas to be rather turbulent. Actually, very few Caribbean islands have enjoyed St. Thomas's long centuries of peace and tran-

quillity. While the two other major islands in the Virgins, St. Croix and St. John, were being burned and pillaged by slave insurrections, St. Thomas, unmolested, went about its business of being host to every kind of ship and sailor on the open seas.

Every West Indian island has its share of romantic ruins; St. Thomas has comparatively few, and most of its buildings have been in use for centuries. Modern shops in Charlotte Amalie, the capital, occupy the premises of warehouses that were built more than a hundred years ago. These have been restored, partially or completely, revealing soaring arches, floorings of Spanish tile and marble, and thick walls that provide a kind of natural air-conditioning system. In the shops, myriad imported silver, china, silk, and other luxury items are on sale.

St. Thomas occupies some 32 square miles of island space, which juts out from the sea to a height of 1,500 feet. There are more than 30 hotels, modern shopping centers, a large yacht marina, and some of the gayest night life in the Caribbean – in addition to all the other

ANEGADA

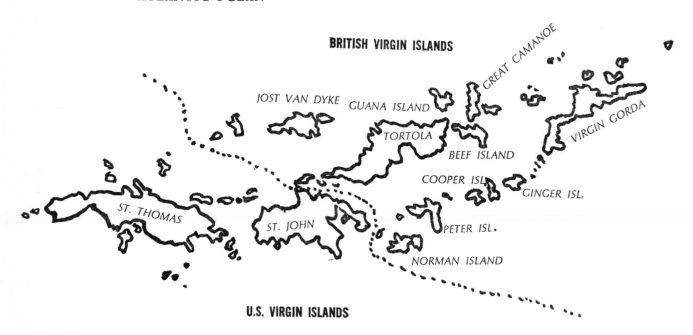

ATLANTIC OCEAN

BRITISH VIRGIN ISLANDS

GREAT CAMANOE

JOST VAN DYKE GUANA ISLAND

VIRGIN GORDA

TORTOLA

BEEF ISLAND

COOPER ISL.

GINGER ISL.

ST. THOMAS

ST. JOHN

PETER ISL.

NORMAN ISLAND

U.S. VIRGIN ISLANDS

CARIBBEAN SEA

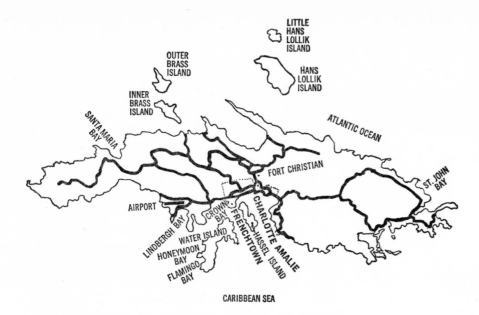

LITTLE HANS LOLLIK ISLAND

OUTER BRASS ISLAND

HANS LOLLIK ISLAND

INNER BRASS ISLAND

SANTA MARIA BAY

ATLANTIC OCEAN

FORT CHRISTIAN

ST. JOHN BAY

AIRPORT

CROWN BAY

FRENCHTOWN

LINDBERGH BAY

WATER ISLAND

HONEYMOON BAY

HASSEL ISLAND

CHARLOTTE AMALIE

FLAMINGO BAY

CARIBBEAN SEA

an Africanized quadrille and Irish jigs are seen everywhere.

St. Thomas, along with the other American Virgins, was purchased by the United States from Denmark in 1917 at a price of $25,000,000 or 48 tons of gold, one of the wisest national investments ever made. The economic growth of St. Thomas can only be called dramatic: income-tax collections have quadrupled, revenue from customs has increased 2,000 percent, and imports from 48 countries exceed $45 million a year. About half a million tourists visit here every year, and almost 90 percent of them go no farther than St. Thomas. Catering to tourists are a wide variety of beachfront and hilltop hotels ranging from the ultraluxurious to the simple *pension*. St. Thomas is still trying to catch up with the tourist tidal wave that has inundated the island.

outdoor sun-time activities one would expect, such as swimming, snorkeling, water skiing, skin diving, fishing, boating, tennis, and the like.

The capital, Charlotte Amalie, is spread over three hills named by sailors of an earlier century for the three masts of a ship – top, main, and mizzen – but now called Denmark, Synagogue, and Government Hills. The charm of the city lies mainly in the narrow alleys, ancient warehouses, shopping lanes bordered with tropical flowers, and old walls hung with bougainvillea. One of the most magnificent views in all the Caribbean is to be had from Skyline Drive, which overlooks the town and harbor of the capital.

Among the signal sights of interest are the seventeenth-century Fort Christian, the gravestones of old cemeteries – Danish, Military, Catholic, and Jewish – Market Square on an early Saturday morning, the Frederick Evangelical Lutheran Church, second oldest of that denomination in the New World, and a famous old synagogue. Although the countryside has no particular historic site to offer (one should, however, stop and visit Bluebeard's Castle, now developed into one of the best hotels of the island), the beauty of landscape and seascape from almost every point of view is ravishing.

Carnival time finds the streets of Charlotte Amalie athrob with the rhythm of steel bands and glowing with the color of strange hats and costumes. The entire population participates, and certain folklore dances such as

ST. CROIX
(U.S. Virgin Islands)

In a Nutshell:

An island of tranquillity and old-world charm, particularly evident in its capital, Christiansted. Size: 84 square miles. Good roads, beautiful beaches, excellent hotel accommodations. Golf, fishing, horseback riding, water skiing, horse racing, cockfights. Good airline connections with the United States, Canada, South America, and Mexico, St. Thomas, Puerto Rico, and the other Caribbean Islands, Language: English.

Only forty miles of water separate St. Croix and St. Thomas, but they are worlds apart in atmosphere and tempo. Where St. Thomas is mountainous and ultrascenic, St. Croix features fertile, low-lying lands and lovely hideaway beaches. If St. Thomas gives the impression of being chic, smart, and very much part of this century, St. Croix fills the traveler with a feeling of stepping back in time to an era of leisurely, lazy candlelight living.

St. Croix, 28 miles long by 10 miles wide, is the largest of the three major American Virgins. Its in-

St. Croix is a favorite with writers and artists, and there is an element of the upper bohemia to be found there, but on a much quieter scale than in St. Thomas. Generally, the old-time residents are rather conservative and would like to retain the quiet and pleasant way of life to which they are accustomed. There is little night life on the island and hardly any exuberant revelry. But St. Croix has too many charms to withstand the encroachments of tourism. The number of visitors to this "Garden of the Antilles" is increasing every year. Residents and visitors succumb naturally to the attractions of the outdoor life on and in the sea, at St. Croix's numerous lovely beaches, in the placid and translucent surf, and on waters that teem with fish life.

A host of resorts, inns, and hotels have recently cropped up to accommodate the ever-increasing number of tourists. What is more important is the island's partly flat terrain, which made it particularly amenable to the construction of a jet airport. This makes possible direct flights from the continent.

Buck Island (Reef National Monument)

This island, just off the coast of St. Croix, was designated a National Monument because of the barrier reef that surrounds the eastern part of it. In the clear lagoon between the island and the reef are remarkable formations of elkhorn, staghorn, and brain coral, with colorful fish and other interesting marine life. Buck Island, just a mile long and about 300 feet high, is easily reached from Christiansted.

ST. JOHN
(U.S. Virgin Islands)

In a Nutshell:

Romantic, mountainous island with interesting historical background. Size: 21 square miles. One third of the island is a National Park. Beautiful tropical vegetation, good beaches, and few but excellent accommodations. Accessible from St. Thomas by boat (3 miles). Language: English.

habitants are called *Crusians* or *Cruzans*. The capital retains its Danish name, Christiansted. It is difficult to imagine a lovelier West Indian harbor, a living restoration of an eighteenth-century port whose pastel pinks, blues, and yellows give it the appearance of a stage setting. To many, this is simply the most charming town in the West Indies. It has a beautifully preserved old Danish port, everywhere a blaze of bougainvillea and hibiscus. Shops are enclosed beneath cool, breezy arcades that make shopping a pleasure.

Start your exploration of Christiansted at the waterfront and town square, now officially classified as a National Historic Site. Here are the seventeenth-century Dutch Fort Christiansvaern, the Danish post office, public library, original customs house, an old church known as Steeple Building, and Government House. The reception hall of the last-named edifice is decorated with wonderful replicas of original Danish furnishings.

At the western part of the island lies the almost equally beautiful port of Frederiksted, whose pastel-tinted homes of basic Danish design are embroidered with a whole gallery of Victorian architectural motifs: cupolas, galleries of iron and wood, and general gingerbread.

Between Christiansted and Frederiksted the landscape is dotted with old sugar mills and plantation estate houses, some of which, like Sprat Hall, have been converted into hotels. These are today's reminder that St. Croix once compared with Barbados as the richest of the sugar-and-rum islands. The names of these plantations are sometimes as fanciful and attractive as the residence: Whim, Concordia, Wheel of Fortune, Upper Love, Peter's Rest, Little Princess, Judy's Fancy.

St. John is an island for those who wish to escape the infringements of a civilization that is too complex for them. It has been described as "primitive" – but for the tourist, it has a kind of primitiveness that comes with modern plumbing, frigidaires, electricity, radio – and fine accommodations.

St. John's attempts to resist, hitherto, the encroachments of our neon way of life and to maintain its exclusiveness can be traced in great measure to its history. Slightly more than 200 years ago, the island's prospects of becoming the most flourishing of the Virgins, because of its excellent soil and high rainfall, were summarily cut short by a revolution of African slaves that could only be described as horrendous. The Elmina tribe that had been imported here considered that to till the soil was degrading – it was, in their opinion, woman's work. On November 13, 1733, they rose in resentment and massacred every white inhabitant they could lay a machete to. It took six months to restore order, but the decline of St. John from that day on was sealed.

The generations of residents since the rebellion have stoutly held to the simple life of fishing, raising livestock, and burning charcoal, and although in more recent years Laurance Rockefeller has developed a magnificent resort in the Caneel Bay Plantation area, adding more tourist accommodations to those already provided in other good places scattered about, the island is still generally unspoiled.

One third of St. John is taken up with the Virgin Island National Park. All through the island one can see the most impressive ruins of walls and buildings that were once great plantations and are now encrusted with tropical vegetation. Here and there one will see huge sugar caldrons, abandoned centuries before, in which bright flowers bloom.

Today, St. John is still an escapist's paradise. Anyone who wishes to dodge the slings and arrows of our tense and anxiety-ridden civilization for a day, a month, or forever will find a haven of peace and serenity with which few places in the world can compare. In addition, the gleaming beaches and mirror-clear waters are perfect for fishing, swimming, snorkeling, and underwater photography.

This modern Eden is being invaded by more and more visitors every year, by travelers who long for cool, clean air, for the beauties of tropical nature, and for the knowledge that at least one spot on earth will retain forever its pristine, unmarred loveliness.

TORTOLA
(British Virgin Islands)

In a Nutshell:

Beautiful, remote island. Mountain scenery, great beaches, a few good accommodations. Capital: Road Town. Language: English.

Not all the Virgin Islands are American. Almost three dozen of them are British; the major one is called Tortola and is approximately the size of St. Thomas.

If you feel the need to escape almost completely from the hubbub and tensions of cosmopolitan life, then find your way to this oasis of absolute peace and quiet, where there is no traffic, no telephones, cables, radio, or television. There is, however, a weekly newspaper – and several hotels, one of which is built on the ruins of an old fort.

Motorboats and sailboats shuttle back and forth to the capital city, Road Town, from St. Thomas, only three hours away across safe waters. Even though the island is British, the currency used is American, since many of the natives work for the Yankee dollar in St. Thomas. Although still considered rather primitive, Tortola, too, is beginning to enjoy the benefits of tourism as the flood of vacationing escapees to the Virgin Islands expands. For the time being, however, the visitor must be prepared to enjoy the tranquillity of the island without too many of the comforts of home.

Similarly attractive to "escapees" are the other, fancifully named British Virgin Islands – Jost Van Dyke, Virgin Gorda, Beef Island, Great Dog, Cockroach, Fallen Jerusalem, Dead Man's Chest.

Jost Van Dyke was named for a Dutch pirate. The inhabitants are such expert seamen that few learn to swim – or so they claim. Virgin Gorda ("The Fat Virgin") is supposed to be the island that made Columbus remember St. Ursula and her virgin followers. The natural attractions of this island, particularly its marine caves, called "baths" by the natives, will remind you of Capri's Blue Grotto. A luxury resort is situated here, "Little Dix Bay," Laurance Rockefeller having bought one of the enchanting beach sites in which the island abounds. It is rumored that Beef Island as well will soon see the erection of a multimillion-dollar tourist hostelry and gambling casino. It is fairly certain that the unspoiled hills and beaches of the British Virgins will, in the near future, be decked out in the finery of luxury resorts, restaurants, night clubs, and other tourist amenities. In the meantime, the visitor in search of the primitive and simple life will find the British Virgins to be as far removed from the tensions and anxieties of modern life as possible.

SINT MAARTEN-
SAINT MARTIN

In a Nutshell:

A partly Dutch, partly French possession. Free port. Friendly mountain scenery. Dutch capital: Philipsburg. French capital: Marigot. Good fishing and lobster catching, delightful beaches, fine gift shops, excellent accommodations on both parts of the island. Good airline connections with

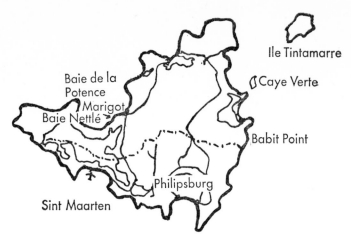

other Caribbean islands. Languages: Dutch and French, also English.

Having discovered the island on St. Martin's day, 1493, Columbus called it San Martino. The Dutch subsequently called it Sint Maarten. The French called it Saint Martin. The Spanish left the island early; the Netherlands and French governments then decided to share the island between them. To draw boundaries, a walking contest was hit upon. Starting from the same point, a Frenchman and a Dutchman walked in opposite directions (unlike the tortoise and the hare). A line was drawn straight across the island from their point of departure to their point of meeting. Since the Frenchman walked faster, the larger part of St. Martin is in French hands. However, the smaller portion left to the Dutch contained valuable salt ponds which made up for the deficiency in area.

History – and particularly European history – is witness to the fact that neighboring countries rarely get on with each other. The exact reverse is true in Saint Martin: there are no border guards, no arguments, and no jealousies, bickerings, or difficulties of any kind. One is tempted to recommend that the United Nations make a study of St. Martin's enviable record of peaceful coexistence. The findings would be of value to the world.

About 3,000 people inhabit the green valleys, green hills, and unspoiled beaches of the Dutch side. The capital of Dutch Sint Maarten is Philipsburg, which occupies a crescent-shaped sandbar between Great Bay and the Great Salt Pond. This unique setting makes Philipsburg one of the Caribbean's most delightful and picturesque sights. Less spectacular is the French capital of Marigot.

1

Jamaica: Calypso Group (Montego Bay)

2
Jamaica: Port Antonio

3
Jamaica: A Beach on the North Shore (Ocho Rios)

Haiti: The Magnificent Waterfalls "Saut d'Eau"

Haiti: The Ruins of Sans-Souci Palace at Milot

<
7
Dominican Republic:
Ruins of the Monastery of St. Francis, Santo Domingo

8
Modern Santo Domingo, Capital of the
Dominican Republic

Puerto Rico: The Fortaleza, Governor's Residence in San Juan

10
*Puerto Rico: History and
Modern Life in San Juan*

11
*Puerto Rico: Castillo de San Felipe
del Morro in San Juan*

12

Tortola (British Virgin Islands)

13

Virgin Islands: A Typical View from Roadtown

14
St. Thomas Aerial Tramway
(U.S. Virgin Islands)

15
Carnival in St. Thomas
(U.S. Virgin Islands)

16

St. Thomas (U.S. Virgin Islands): View of Charlotte Amalie

Christiansted, Capital of St. Croix (U.S. Virgin Islands)

18
*Christiansted, St. Croix
(U.S. Virgin Islands):
Old Danish Government House*

19
*Fort Christianvaern
(St. Croix, U.S. Virgin Islands)*

20
St. Croix (U.S. Virgin Islands):
Ruins of a Plantation

21
St. John
(U.S. Virgin Islands):
Romantic Caneel Bay

22

View overlooking Dutch Sint Maarten: Philipsburg

<
23
St. Kitts (St. Christopher):
Brimstone Hill, Old British Fortification

24
The Island of Saba: An Extinct Volcano

Strolling the Beach at Nevis

Antigua: Historic English Harbour

Antigua: Typical Caribbean Scene, Ruins of a Sugar Mill

Hostelry on Montserrat

29
Place de l'Église, Pointe-à-Pitre, Guadeloupe

30
Guadeloupe: View from Gosier

31
St. Barthélemy: The Capital, Gustavia

32
Welcome to Dominica: Steel Band and Rainbow

34
Martinique:
St. Pierre with Mont Pelée

35
Martinique: Historic Diamond Rock

<
37

St. Lucia: Countryside (Soufrière and Petit Piton)

38

St. Lucia: Harbor of Castries

Barbados: The Careenage at Bridgetown

Barbados: Dunes and Beach

41
Barbados: The coast of St. James
(Sandy Lane)

42
Barbados: Codrington College

>
43
St. Vincent:
View from Sugar Mill Inn
near Kingstown

44

Grenada: The Harbor of St. George's

47
*Trinidad: Hosein,
the Moslem Celebration*

48
*Trinidad:
Santa Cruz Valley*

49
Tobago: Tropical Wonderland

51
Scarborough: Capital of Tobago

52   *The young Flamingos are gray*

53   *The beautiful parent Flamingos*

54   *Just hatched by the warm tropical sun*

55   *Nests, eggs, children, and parents*

Bonaire: Native Flamingo Colony

56
*Curaçao: Heerenstraat in the
Business Center of Willemstad*

57
*Curaçao: The "Floating Market"
in Willemstad*

Airview of Willemstad, Capital of Curaçao

59
The Bluest Waters of the Caribbean Surround Aruba

60
Aruba: Ancient Indian Pottery

61
Leeward Coast of Aruba

Sunset on Grand Cayman

All the waters surrounding the island and the roads across it are used jointly by the French and Dutch without let or hindrance. Both nationalities celebrate each other's national holidays – July 14 (Bastille Day) for the French, April 30 (the Queen's Holiday) for the Dutch.

There are a number of excellent beaches on the island, which are rapidly being developed with an eye to catching the tourist trade. The Little Bay Beach Hotel near Philipsburg, situated on a beautiful beach, features a gambling casino.

Sightseers will want to see the crumbling ruins of Old Fort Amsterdam, once one of the Caribbean's mighty fortresses. The island is full of local color, and the countryside is populated with happy, friendly natives tending their chickens, goats, and donkeys.

The French section contains about six thousand of the nine thousand people of the island. The promotion of tourism has lagged a bit, but of late this portion of the island has taken vigorous steps to broadcast its attractions and its hospitality. It has a quaint charm – and La Majeur Beach, where the powdery white sand has for backdrop a large planting of sea-grape trees and a huge grove of coconut palms.

There are no import duties or excise taxes on the entire island, and it is the freest free port in the Caribbean. You may purchase and take out whatever strikes your fancy from either side of the dividing line without formalities or border guards.

SABA

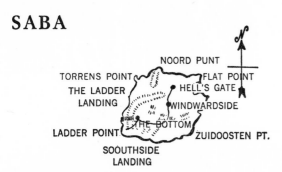

In a Nutshell:

One of the great scenic attractions of the West Indies. Size – 5 square miles. Can be reached from Sint Maarten or St. Kitts. Simple accommodations. Capital: Bottom. Language: English. Population: about 1100.

Only the most intrepid colonizers would have considered settling on Saba. In the first place, this Dutch island is an extinct volcano, only five square miles in area, without anything even remotely resembling a port. There are, indeed, two places to land – Fort Bay, a strip of black-sand beach and rocks, and Ladder Bay, so called because 530 steps mount directly from the shoreline to the island's capital, Bottom.

The vessel that transports you to Saba will anchor off shore in the open sea. Smaller boats will ferry you to Fort Bay, if the sea is smooth, or to Ladder Bay, if the waters are too rough. There is also a small airplane flying to Saba.

Your trip to Saba starts with excitement and adventure, and as you proceed inland there is more of the same to come.

Once you have landed at Fort Bay, a jeep will take you up 800 feet on what seems to be an almost perpendicular road to the quaintly named capital city of Bottom. Bottom looks like a charming European village. It occupies the only flat spot on this vertical island. Guest Houses here are prepared to accommodate visitors. You will be delighted with the cleanliness of the streets and homes and the carefully tended gardens.

From Bottom, you may venture higher to the tinier villages of Windwardside, 1,800 feet high, and Hellsgate, which cling precariously to the mountainside. The view of the steep drop to the ocean on the one side and to the rocky mountains slopes rising high above you on the other leave you fascinated with the idea that people live in such remote and scenic isolation.

You would expect that such an environment would have made the Sabans as flinty as the rock they inhabit. In fact, they are known throughout the West Indies as the "friendliest people in the world."

With no industry, little farming, and some fishing, the problem of making a living is considerable. Most of the men leave the island to work in the great oil refineries of Aruba and Curaçao. The women stay at home and produce exquisite lace, which you can purchase here or in Curaçao.

A new airstrip on Saba made the island's unique attractions more accessible to tourists.

ST. BARTHÉLEMY (ST. BARTS)

In a Nutshell:

French island, dependency of Guadeloupe. Size: Approximately 8 square miles. Location: 15 miles southeast of

St. Martin. Excellent harbor and accommodations. Fishing, snorkeling, sailing, water skiing. Excellent food. Flight connections with St. Martin and Guadeloupe.

St. Barthélemy, usually referred to as St. Barts, may be reached by air from Guadeloupe in one hour, and from St. Martin in ten minutes. Measuring only eight square miles, with a population of about 2,700, mostly descendants of Frenchmen who came to the island in the seventeenth century from Normandy, Brittany, and Poitou, St. Barts is a quiet, pastoral island, the only Antillean island with a Swedish contribution to its

character. The French were the first to colonize St. Barts, but in 1784 they ceded it to Sweden in exchange for trading rights in Göteborg. Sweden returned it to France in 1877, but during the period of Swedish rule its capital had acquired the name Gustavia, after Gustavus III, and that is still its name.

St. Barts has much to offer: the finest harbor in the Caribbean, an unsurpassed beach, and so much charm that its seeming isolation may soon be a thing of the past.

ST. KITTS (ST. CHRISTOPHER)

In a Nutshell:

Volcanic island with interesting history and impressive historical monuments. Basseterre is the capital. Size – 68 square miles, 40,000 inhabitants. Good airline connections with the United States, Canada, and other Caribbean islands. Tennis, fishing, hunting, horseback riding. Language: English.

Everyone feels so affectionately toward the island of St. Christopher that to call it other than by its appealing diminutive, St. Kitts, is today unthinkable.

Its pride and popularity lie in the fact that St. Kitts is considered the "Mother Colony of the British West Indies." Settled by the English in 1623, St. Kitts served as a base from which many of the other West Indian islands were later colonized.

The French and English struggled for control of St. Kitts for more than 150 years, and although the English finally won out, Gallic influence is found in the name of the capital, Basseterre (not to be confused with the capital of the same name in Guadeloupe) and in the French iron-grillwork decorations found on many old public and private buildings.

Basseterre is a busy West Indian port that seems to have stepped out of an eighteenth-century mezzotint. Schooners from Antigua, St. Martin, Montserrat, and other neighboring islands criss-cross in the port area with freighters from Great Britain, Canada, and the United States.

Exquisite examples of old colonial architecture are to be found in Basseterre's Government House, Old Court House, and many examples of fine Georgian colonial private homes. All the main streets of the capital lead to a central area called the Circus, with its tall Victorian clock tower and fountain, which look like something out of an Andersen fairy tale.

Although not yet developed as a resort island, St. Kitts does offer the visitor some fairly good beaches, which will probably be improved as tourism increases, interesting rock formations of twisted volcanic lava, and a lovely cloud-shrouded mountain peak, Mt. Misery

(4,314 feet). St. Kitts also boasts an airport at Golden Rock, a mile from the capital.

The most impressive sight on the island is Brimstone Hill Fortress, "The Gibraltar of the West." The ramparts of the gigantic stone-and-mortar military installation rise more than 700 feet from the ocean in apparent impregnability, an engineering feat that later served to inspire Henri Christophe to build the Citadelle in Haiti.

The view from the heights, especially when framed by the fortress's colonial archways, will take your breath away. Outlined against the horizon and set off by the blue waters of the Caribbean are the islands of St. Eustatius, Saba, St. Martin, Montserrat, and St. Barthélemy. Sugar cane and cotton plantations dot the inland landscape.

Volcanic Mt. Misery is a constant attraction to mountain climbers, although its name would seem to callenge the most dauntless, and the picturesque countryside and scenic rockbound coast are the perfect settings for picnic outings and hiking excursions.

NEVIS

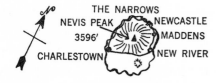

In a Nutshell:

Small, interesting volcanic island close to St. Kitts, from which it can be reached by launch or plane. Fine beaches, good accommodations. A quiet island off the beaten path. Language: English.

The birthplace of Alexander Hamilton is a mountainous Caribbean paradise that has so far withstood the rising tide of West Indian tourism. How much longer the gentle and basically friendly people of Nevis can hold out against those outside interests that have an eye on the island's beautiful coral beaches and eighteenth-century historical remains is questionable. The fact remains that this idyllic little island-in-the-sun has a multitude of charms to attract tourists in great quantities.

Columbus called the island Las Nievas (The Snows). From a distance, the white clouds that hover over the mountaintops do resemble snow-capped peaks. Rising dramatically from the sea, only two miles from its sister island of St. Kitts, Nevis is ruggedly volcanic in origin and aspect. Forest-clad slopes descend right into the water or to palm-tree-studded beaches. The highest point is Nevis Peak (3,596 feet), in the center of the island, which is joined to Hurricane Hill (1,192 feet) and Saddle Hill (1,432 feet).

Those who enjoy the *dolce far niente* of tropical living will find that Nevis more than lives up to their tastes, for there are no tourist shopping places here, no night life to speak of, and no ostentatious resorts. The pace is so leisurely, unhurried, and unharried that one is completely unmindful of the passing of time. One day drifts into another as you spend your time picnicking, fishing, or exploring the island for Carib Indian remains.

Colonial history is here in full bloom, and you will see, among the rarer flowers, Fig Tree Church, where Nelson married Fanny Nesbit two centuries ago. The tattered church register contains their signatures. In Charlestown, the foundations of the house in which Alexander Hamilton was born in 1757 are still standing. American visitors are particularly attracted to this spot, although they may be surprised to learn that the famous American patriot was the illegitimate son of James Hamilton and Rachel Levine, a fact often overlooked in American history books.

Other interesting objectives for sightseers are the 200-year-old Bath House and its thermal baths, which one can still sample. In the eighteenth century, this was a luxury establishment. It is being restored and renovated and may enjoy again some of the glories of its earlier history. St. Thomas's Church is the oldest on the island. The churchgrounds contain interesting ancient tombstones.

The quaint and colorful waterfront of Charlestown usually marks the beginning and end of every tour of historical Nevis.

ANTIGUA

In a Nutshell:

A typically English island, size – 108 square miles, excellent airline connections with the United States, Canada, Europe, South America, and the other Caribbean islands. Beautiful beaches, interesting scenery, famous historical monuments (English Harbour). Golf, tennis, hunting (deer, ducks, pigeons), boating and yachting (for hire), deep-sea fishing. Capital: St. John's. Very good hotel and resort accommodations. Language: English.

The inhabitants call their island An-tée-ga. You will probably call it a "jolly fine bit of paradise," particularly if you have spent enough time here to absorb the very British mannerisms of speech of this very British Caribbean island.

Antigua's cultivated countryside and rolling hills resemble any of England's southern shires, except that

here sugar and cotton replace the less exotic agricultural products of the Mother Country.

If the foregoing gives you the impression that Antigua is rather British, we have understated the case. The islanders are, to the outsider, almost excessively English – and proud of it. For they are, in a sense, heirs to the glories of Lord Nelson, who captained his fleet at Antigua's famous English Harbor.

Standing here is Nelson's Dockyard, where His Majesty's ships were refitted to sail against France in the decisive naval conflict of the Napoleonic Wars. To enter these precincts is to step back in time almost two centuries. You will discover the home that Nelson occupied with his bride, the widow Nesbit (it is called the Admiral's House), old cannons and caldrons used for boiling pitch, and a variety of remains dating back to the eighteenth century.

A magnificent view of Nelson's Dockyard is obtained from Shirley Heights, above the harbor. On these heights are the ruins of the barracks of the fortress that protected the area, of which long lines of walls and arches, now in the process of restoration, stand as mute sentinels and monuments of Britain's naval greats – Nelson, Hood, and Rodney.

Today, English Harbour is a rendezvous of yachtsmen, since its almost circular shape is completely protected from the open sea. Flags of many nations fly from yachts that anchor here.

Antigua's salubrious climate is dry and sunny, and even the summer heat is tempered by cool trade winds and the low humidity. The coastline alternates rocky indentations with magnificent beaches for a variety of views that is never monotonous.

The capital city, St. John's, is a typical West Indian port, where schooners from all parts of the Caribbean dock, creating a tropical profusion (some say confusion) of local color. Antiguans are among the friendliest people in the West Indies; their houses and gardens are extremely neat and well kept.

As a consequence of being favored by nature, Antigua was selected as the "perfect hideaway" by a group of wealthy American escapists. They leased a wilderness and created a resort colony called The Mill Reef Club, complete with luxury homes, roads, landscaping, and a central club building for their personal pleasures. Whether this has set the tone for Antigua's resorts or not, the fact remains that, generally speaking, the island's hostelries are high class.

MONTSERRAT

In a Nutshell:

Small, peaceful island. Size – 33 square miles. Mountain scenery, good accommodations, golf, tennis, fine beaches, fishing, airline connections with Antigua. Language: English.

If you can picture West Indians of African descent speaking English with a decided Irish brogue, then you won't be surprised when you land in Montserrat. But this is rarely the case with visitors, who are rather startled at hearing the Afro-Irish accent of native residents who bear such Gaelic names as Sweeney and Galaway.

The island was originally settled by a group of Irishmen who had first settled on St. Kitts, but, unable to bear their English brethren, struck out for the golden beaches of Montserrat.

Although small and rather rocky, the island is quite fertile and produces wonderful mangoes, avocadoes, breadnuts – and tasty rum punches flavored with home-grown limes. Cotton and tomatoes are the two staple products that have a market outside the island. There are lush green forests, clear streams, and several attractive waterfalls. There are also several fine beaches, some white, some volcanic black or gray.

A regular airline service reaches Montserrat, but a preferred way of visiting the island is to take one of the many trading schooners that skip over the 27 miles from Antigua to Montserrat's main town and capital, Plymouth. The road that leads from Plymouth will take you to a plantation house called Woodlands Estate and from there into a steep valley charmingly called Soldier's Gut. Here the English and French massacred each other in a bid for ownership of the island two centuries ago.

Among sports that can be practiced or watched are golf and tennis—and cricket, which goes over big with the natives. Hunting the giant frog is also something of a pastime, as this very edible crapaud is a tasty dish when prepared Montserrat-style. It is locally known as "mountain chicken."

Mountainous Montserrat is far enough off the beaten path to attract many a tourist, it has good accommodations, and the word is out that the government and its citizens are preparing to develop the island's tourist potential. There are several attractive real-estate developments.

GUADELOUPE

In a Nutshell:

Large French double island. 583 square miles. Capital: Basse-Terre, in the mountainous part; larger city is Pointe-à-Pitre with good harbor. Excellent airline connections with North and South America, Europe, and other Caribbean islands. Fine hotel accommodations. Sailing (yacht clubs), tennis, fishing, guided mountain climbing, cockfights. Language: French. Population: 300,000.

Guadeloupe was named by Columbus for the famous monastery of Guadeloupe in Estremadura. The Spanish were not successful here, and after a hundred years or so they abandoned the island to the French, who colonized it, spent hundreds of years disputing ownership with the English, and finally incorporated it as a full-fledged department of France.

In geographic outline, Guadeloupe resembles a butterfly whose outstretched wings lie upon the blue waters of the Caribbean. It is, in fact, two islands divided by a narrow channel called the Salée River. The northeastern island is called Grande-Terre, and its main city, Pointe-à-Pitre, is situated right on the Rivière Salée. This part of Guadeloupe is rather flat, fertile, and devoted to agriculture. The southern part, which lies across a drawbridge, is the other island of Basse-Terre. Despite its name, which means "low land," the area is very mountainous. Some peaks reach more than 4,500 feet into the sky (La Soufrière, 4,870 feet: Sans-Toucher, 4,855). The political capital of the island is here, and it, too, is called Basse-Terre.

Pointe-à-Pitre is the commercial center of the islands that constitute Guadeloupe. The high points of any sightseeing here are visits to the Iron Cathedral, composed entirely of bits and pieces of iron welded or bolted together, and the colorful little harbor. The low-lying countryside of Grande-Terre is of interest if you are concerned with seeing sugar cane plantations. However, the beaches that surround this part of Guadeloupe are among the most beautiful to be found, and the one at Ste.-Anne is really for sun worshipers.

While on Grande-Terre, visit La Pergola du Gosier, which is an exceptionally fine French restaurant. Bungalows, called Pergolettes, and a terrace dining room overlook a beautiful shaded beach and little out islands, providing a view that has attracted more than one artist.

On the northern tip of Grande-Terre is the beach at Moule, often referred to as the "Beach of Skulls." The Caribs, English, and French fought many a battle on this shore, and many who fell were buried in the dunes back of the beach. The tides have uncovered some of the graves, and one is likely to stumble over skulls and bones as one goes bathing off a beach that would otherwise be ideal.

Then there is the charming village of St. François, with another fine beach, where almost all the populace devote their lives to fishing.

Pointe des Châteaux, on the southeast point of the island, provides the most stirring view in all Guadeloupe and is an inspiration for many artists and photographers. Enormous rocks jut out into the surf, and the seas seem angry as they cast their foam high and wide. An illusion exists, in that the island of La Désirade seems within a stone's throw but is actually six miles away. A giant cross at one end serves as guardian over the island.

On the island of Basse-Terre the scenery is simply spectacular. Volcanic peaks brood over a landscape that is filled with rushing streams (there are more than seventy here), rain forests, and tropical vegetation of all kinds. As you ascend into the mountains, you will discover a village of East Indians at Matouba. It is reported that ancient rites performed by these inhabitants still include the sacrifice of animals. At Trois-Rivières, you will see rocks that bear Carib Indian inscriptions. The Capital, Basse-Terre city, with a population of 15,000, is situated on the southwest coast of the island Basse-Terre. It is an attractive city, with its new General de Gaulle Boulevard, its government buildings, Schoelcher Monument, the huge old fort St. Charles, the seventeenth-century cathedral, and a handsome residential section. Also it is the banana harbor for the island, and banana boats may be seen along the extensive pier. On the east coast of Grande-Terre nestles Le Moule, with about 15,000 inhabitants.

Between Pointe-à-Pitre and Basse-Terre a magnificent scenic road, with lush vegetation and fine vistas, winds between the sea and the mountains, passing through the picturesque towns of Petit-Bourg, Goyave, Capesterre, Trois-Rivières, Dole, and Gourbeyre.

Sports of all kinds will enliven your holiday hours in Guadeloupe. Both Pointe-à-Pitre and Basse-Terre have tennis, bridge, and yacht clubs. Soccer and cockfighting are the favorite spectator sports, and, of course, beach pleasure can be had almost anywhere.

DOMINICA

In a Nutshell:

An unspoiled mountain island with many rivers and beautiful tropical vegetation. Size – 305 square miles. Capital: Roseau. Good hotel accommodations. Home of the remaining Carib Indians in the West Indies. Sailing, tennis, fishing, hunting. Air connections with the United States, Puerto Rico, and neighboring islands. Languages: French and English.

On this island dwell the last of the Carib Indians, a scant 600 of the many thousands that populated most of the West Indies before the arrival of Columbus.

Ruggedly wild, forest-clad, and unspoiled is the terrain of Dominica. Forests of mahogany, cedar, bamboo, mango, and palm cover the almost vertical landscape. The mountains are so high they can be seen from Martinique, 30 miles south, or Guadeloupe, 30 miles north. The highest peak is Morne Diablotin (4,747 feet). Despite the fact that Dominica has an airstrip and there are good connections between this and other islands in the Caribbean, there is a feeling of isolation and remoteness about Dominica that has been a drawback to its tourist development.

Only the persistent Dominicans could have built a road across this mountainous island. But the Transinsular Road, as it is called, offers the most breathtaking natural scenery in all the West Indies. Steep cliffs, cascading rivers, jungle mazes, tropical rain forests, and seascapes of incredible loveliness with waves dashing furiously against the rockbound coast fill the eye and daze the senses.

The less ambitious sightseer will be content with the shorter trips available around the capital, Roseau. The Botanical Gardens are among the loveliest in the Caribbean. About four miles from Roseau are the twin waterfalls of Layou and Pagoua, which provide a romantic setting for picnics. A visit to the lime plantation in Morne Valley, the home of Rose's Lime Juice, is a pleasant stopping-off point for an hour's relaxation.

Dominica is recommended to the adventurous traveler. Although there are some beautiful beaches, these are mostly deserted. Night life is nonexistent, and few facilities for fishing or boating are organized. However, the photographer, with an eye for nature at its wildest, can have a field day in Dominica.

MARTINIQUE

In a Nutshell:

Large French island. Mountain scenery, volcanoes, beautiful vegetation. Capital is Fort-de-France, a good harbor. Size: 425 square miles with about 330,000 inhabitants. Very good hotel accommodations, fine beaches. Sailing, fishing, hunting, tennis, cockfights. Excellent airline connections with other Caribbean islands. Language: French.

Martinique, an island endowed with great natural beauty, is the glamorous and temperamental "Queen of the Antilles," largest and northernmost of the little Windward Islands. Originally populated solely by the Carib Indians, those ubiquitous natives of the Caribbean, this lush and lovely island was briefly visited in 1502 by Christopher Columbus. Accorded an enthusiastically hostile reception by his unwilling hosts, Columbus in his hasty departure was accompanied by a hail of arrows which precluded his naming of another discovery. Even so, it is a fair assumption that Colum-

bus could not have improved on the romantic name by which the Caribs knew their home – Island of Flowers, or Madinina, later to be gallicized as Martinique.

The Carib appellation is still appropriate, because Martinique is a garden filled with flowering hibiscus, bougainvillea, orchids, and other tropical blooms. There is, however, more than flowers to see in Martinique. Plantations produce sugar cane, vanilla, coffee, cocoa; there are forests of mahogany and great salt fields; factories produce some of the best rum in the West Indies. It is also the site of the Pompeii of the New World.

On May 7, 1902, Martinique had two major cities – St.-Pierre and Fort-de-France. On the following day there was only one. Mont Pelée, a volcano, had exploded, wiping out St.-Pierre and its 30,000 inhabitants. The sole survivor was a prisoner who was occupying a dungeon cell. This disaster is recorded in mementoes contained in Dr. Frank Perret Musée Volcanologique, where petrified human and animal remains as well as on-the-spot photographs of the ruined city are kept. In these days of potential atomic destruction, a visit to St.-Pierre is a gruesome reminder of the horrors that nature – or man – can inflict upon humanity.

Fort-de-France is the capital of Martinique and the French West Indies. It is a pure operetta setting with a semicircular harbor containing Fort St. Louis on one side, a green park in the center, and yellow buildings and sidewalk cafés on the other. An interesting married couple of rivers bisects the town – Rivière Madame on the north – Rivière Monsieur on the south.

Across the bay at Trois Îlets was born that famous Creole lady who was to become Empress of France – Josephine Bonaparte. The ruins of her birthplace and the little Beauharnais Museum are great tourist attractions.

Politically, Martinique is probably the most sophisticated of all the Caribbean islands. Since 1946 it has been a department of France, with a prefect and all the rights and privileges of metropolitan France. Composed of thirty-four communes, Martinique enforces a social legislation that is faithfully French, providing social security, free medical care for the poor, and allowances to large families. School attendance is about ninety-five percent, owing to the large number of primary schools in the villages and hamlets.

That Martinique is still French, as enamored of its past as a new millionaire, is due to the whim of a king. Martinique resentfully sustained British occupation during the Seven Years' War between France and England, when it was bandied back and forth between the two great powers as a colonial bauble. But at the Treaty of Paris in 1763 – the year Josephine, the future Empress of France, was born in Martinique – Louis XV gave away Canada, "a few snowy acres," rather than the West Indies.

This decision was most fortunate for America. During the American War of Independence, Admiral de Grasse used Fort-de-France as the base of operations for his fleet, the French sailing from there to Yorktown to aid in the Revolution's most decisive victory.

But the British continued in their determination to claim the little French "Queen of the Antilles." Just south of Fort-de-France lies Rocher du Diamant, a gemlike volcano upcropping from the sea, rising sheer to an altitude of 573 feet.

Following orders of Sir Samuel Hood, Commodore of the Leeward Island stations, the British occupied the rock on January 7, 1804. Manned by 110 sailors and marines under the command of Lieutenant, later Captain, Y. W. Maurice, the rock remained in the hands of the British for about seventeen months, falling to the French on June 29, 1805, in a highly dramatic encounter. The French were able to storm the coastline of the rock and take over the first level under heavy fire. The British retreated to the second level and finally had to seek refuge in the isolation of the top stage of the new fortifications of the lonely rock. In a short time it became evident that their situation was hopeless, and Maurice waved the white flag of surrender.

The irony of this capitulation was that, had Maurice and his gallant band held on, they would have been relieved by Admiral Nelson, whose fleet was only hours away. But by the time Nelson's armada reached the scene, the French were on their way home with their prisoners.

Today, the rugged and fascinating eyrie that is Rocher du Diamant can be visited via *gommier* from the town of Diamant. The 2.4-mile crossing is often rough and difficult, but the rewards of such a visit are in finding the ruins of cisterns and batteries with cannons and cannon balls – all that remains of the one-time British fortress.

On the northwest coast of Martinique is one of the island's most fascinating villages. Off the beaten path, but more than worth the effort, Le Prêcheur is only 6.8 miles from St.-Pierre. One of the oldest parishes on the island, attended only by her fishermen and small-time farmers, Le Prêcheur slumbers peacefully in the dotage of a dazzling past. Here, in a small area named after an islet that resembles a preacher in a pulpit, the haughty Duparquet was rejected in a popular revolt among the Prêchotins. There is a monument to Duparquet – and, paradoxically, only a plaque to the much-admired Françoise d'Aubigné, who became Madame de Maintenon and the second wife of Louis XIV. Only a seventeenth-century spire and the scattered ruins of once-great plantation houses – the survivors of Mont Pelée's violence – now evoke an image of a time gone by, before one of the world's most macabre and fascinating tragedies occurred.

It is during Carnival that visitors are most impressed with the essentially Creole character of their Martiniquan hosts. The indigenous cultures of the island display their proud "party manners" at this time – each group competing with all the other groups in a joyful burst of pride in their ethnic traditions. And it is during Carnival that the true enchantment of this island's Adams and Eves is most prone to afflict the visitor with jealousy. The Martiniquan's ageless sophistication, his simplicity and built-in gaiety devastatingly diminish the visitor's sense of self-importance.

Carnival time is a fantastic spectacle. In the early morning of Ash Wednesday more than 25,000 *diablesses* prowl the streets and *allées* of Fort-de-France, grotesque in their starkly dramatic costumes of black and white, with wigs, masks, headdresses, and even make-up – all in dead black and ghostly white. By midmorning, Martinique is the Middle Ages revisited, with generous applications of demon rum enlivening this most solemn occasion. All day the wake continues, for this is the day that Vaval, or Bois-Bois, king of the carnival, must die. Devils mourn, *cortèges* preempt the narrow streets, musicians contribute dirges or the lilting melodies of the beguine as the spirit moves them, and, georgeously somber in costume and mien, the *diablesses* insist their hearts are broken. Mardi Gras is ending, twenty-four hours later than anywhere else in the world.

Dramatic as it is, the last day of Carnival is merely a sensitive and poetic climax to Mardi Gras – Shrove Tuesday – when hundreds of little "devils" in skin-tight red costumes flourish their gilded tridents and dance along behind the bespangled bigger devils, following the gorgeous floats and the "vidés," bands that play tunes about the Devil and the soon-to-be-deceased Vaval (King Bois-Bois). So pass the last two days of Martinique's annual madness, which from mid-January has been an almost ceaseless festival–with contests and competitions, magnificent costumes, and deliriously wonderful music.

When you are not busy watching the revelers, take a moment to examine the buildings around you here in the capital. The city and its architecture will remind you of the Latin Quarter of New Orleans, especially in the French iron grillwork that adorns the houses.

As for the rest of the island, it is so lush and verdant that one can easily imagine Paul Gauguin painting here – which he did. Palm-fringed beaches are colorful and plentiful on both the north and south shores. Just north of Fort-de-France, a wonderful auto road winds through the center of Martinique's remarkable rain forest and continues to Morne Rouge. Magnificent trees, mountain scenery, exotic vegetation in endless variety, tree-like ferns and low-growing ones, certain rare palms, Bromeliads – all these render the road a modern-day fairyland. In the background, Mont Pelée stands, as always, subdued but not extinct, reminding her subjects occasionally of her existence by such polite explosions as those of 1929 and 1932. From Morne Rouge, this fascinating mountain may be climbed and descended in about eight hours, round trip.

Gay, generous, and completely charming, the people of Martinique are captivating. Their music, customs, and traditions are in perfect harmony with their incomparably beautiful surroundings. Their physical grace, natural adaptability, and subtle sensuality are so exactly attuned to the lovely land they live in that the most casual visitor leaves Martinique with the inexplicable feeling that he has been there before . . . sometime, somewhere. And even the most blasé traveler ponders the ancient conundrum of the anthropologists: does a land create its people in its own image – or do the people mold their surroundings to fit their own collective personality?

In either case, it is impossible to deny that Martinique is "a love you cannot ever leave" or to argue with the emotional Napoleon, who said, "I hold Martinique dear for more reasons than one."

ST. LUCIA

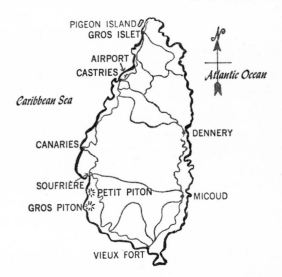

In a Nutshell:

Enchanting island, comparatively quiet. Size – 238 square miles. Outstanding mountain scenery, good harbors and fine beaches. Fishing (tuna, marlin, dolphin, tarpon), tennis, boating. Therapeutic sulphur springs. Capital: Castries. Excellent hotel accommodations. Good airline connections with the United States, Canada, South America, and other Caribbean islands. Languages: English and French. Population: 100,000.

Historians claim that Columbus first sighted this rugged and mountainous island in the sun on St. Lucia's Day (December 13) in 1502. It is also a historical fact that the French and English disputed ownership for hundreds of years (the island changed hands between them fourteen times), accounting for St. Lucia's split personality, with its heritage of British government and French culture.

In more recent years, St. Lucia has been discovered in a way that Spanish conquistadores, French buccaneers, and English colonizers never suspected. This microcosm of all that is beautiful in the Caribbean is now being explored by energetic and adventurous tourists in search of a life as remotely different from their normal, harried existence as possible – in natural surroundings where every view is unique and enchanting and the atmosphere is conducive to the cure of ulcers and nervous disturbances. This they will surely find in St. Lucia.

The island lies between St. Vincent to the south and Martinique to the north – 238 square miles of mountainous landscape shot through with the riotous color of hibiscus, oleander, bougainvillea, flamboyant trees, orchids, and other tropical blooms too numerous to list.

The major city and capital is Castries, a port that permits large ships to sail right up to its wharves across dark lagoon waters. The city unfortunately lost much of its colonial and Victorian flavor when it was burned out in the giant conflagration of 1948. It resembles today almost any modern suburb. Two large hills, one on either side, called La Morne Fortune and La Vigie, hover protectively over the town. Atop the former are the ruins of the eighteenth-century fortifications of Fort Charlotte. The view from here, which encompasses the harbor, is breathtakingly beautiful, particularly at sunset. The highlight of any visit to St. Lucia is a visit to the active volcano of La Soufrière. This is the only drive-in volcano known to us; one can drive a car almost to the lip of the steaming, sulphurous crater and then walk down into the depths to watch the bubbling waters and hissing jets of steam. The nearby sulphur baths have been in use since 1785, when they were used by the troops of Louis XVI. They are famous still for their therapeutic properties.

Two of the most famous landmarks in the Caribbean are the twin peaks of Gros Piton and Petit Piton, which rise straight out of the sea in the southwestern corner of St. Lucia. These are a favorite with local and visiting

mountain climbers, although scaling the heights of the Pitons will never become a general pastime for the less energetic.

Sightseeing in St. Lucia should include beautiful Vigie Beach and Reduit Beach, opposite historic Pigeon Island, which enjoys almost complete isolation and is considered to be very fashionable. Not the least of St. Lucia's charms are the extraordinary seventeenth-century garments worn by the native women, which are almost as colorful as the fabulous costumes donned at Carnival. And, of course, at Mardi Gras, the general air of gaiety that pervades St. Lucia is at its peak.

No longer can St. Lucia be considered one of the sleeping beauties of the Caribbean, for tourists all over the world are now attracted to its tropical magnificence, evidence of which is found in the expanding tourist facilities, now being constructed in many of the island's most scenic settings.

BARBADOS

In a Nutshell:

Hilly island with elegant resorts and hotels (more than 1,000 rooms). Beautiful beaches. Capital is Bridgetown with deep-water harbor. Size – 166 square miles. Golf courses, yacht club, tennis, excellent fishing (wahoo, dolphin, bonito, tarpon, tuna). Famous for flying fish. Airline connections with North and South America, Europe, and other Caribbean islands. Language: English. Population: 250,000.

Comparatively small, Barbados (166 square miles) is an English garden transplanted to the tropics. The quiet, cultivated countryside resembles the mother country's southern shires, Devon or Kent, with their rolling hills and bowers and patchwork of carefully tended fields.

English to the core, Barbadians are proud of the fact that they are considered even "more British than Britain herself." Cricket, high tea, Anglican village churches, and English place names (Yorkshire, Windsor, Hastings) contribute to the anglicized character of Barbados. And Bridgetown, the capital, has a Trafalgar Square with a statue of Lord Nelson that antedates the London statue by 27 years.

The old-world charm of the capital is best explored on foot. The careenage docks are filled with vessels from St. Vincent, St. Lucia, Martinique, and Dominica. Mauby women, so called for the mauby-bark beer they sell, circulate among the stevedores. Harbor policemen are dressed in bell-bottom trousers, white pullover shirts, and flat straw boaters with black bands – imitations of Nelson's sailors. All in all, the port looks today very much as it must have to George Washington, who visited here in 1751.

Bridgetown is a busy little city filled with a bustling population. A more heterogeneous and picturesque group would be hard to find anywhere. Well-dressed planters and businessmen rub elbows with Portuguese merchants. Venezuelan oilmen, turbaned Hindus, and handsome Negro men and women form as cosmopolitan a society as you are likely to find on any Caribbean island.

There are few outstanding sights in the city, but one should certainly visit the house occupied by George Washington, called the "George Washington House," and St. Michael's Cathedral, whose memorial tablets go back to the seventeenth century. The Barbados Museum in Garrison, just a mile out of town, provides the visitor with a wealth of historical data on Barbados.

Start your tour of Barbados from Bridgetown. The roads are mostly paved and, though rather narrow, are quite good. A visit to Sam Lord's Castle, one of the great estate houses built in 1830, is indicaed on all maps. This has now become an outstanding resort, with ex-quisite bedrooms filled with antique heirlooms in the main house. There is a beautiful beach.

Farther north, the cliffs rise sharply on this rocky, windward side of the island. The view is panoramic, and the surf pounds the rocks with tremendous force.

Bathsheba is halfway up the east coast. This is where you will see "the flying fishes play." Try to time your arrival to coincide with the return of the Flying Fish Fleet, famous in the Caribbean. Inland from Bathsheba are the beautiful Scottish Highlands of Barbados, where the "Redlegs" live. The term is derived from the bare knees displayed by the kilted Scots. The Redlegs are the blonde, blue-eyed descendants of early indentured white servants who were sold into slavery after an unsuccessful rebellion against James II of England.

Mahogany and casuarina trees adorn the landscape. Occasionally you will sight a wild monkey or two gamboling from tree to tree. Old windmills, once used for grinding sugar cane, give evidence of the still-prosperous sugar industry. Farley Hill, now a complete ruin, was built in the eighteenth century. The house was used in the filming of Hollywood's *Island in the Sun*.

The road west across the island from Farley Hill leads directly to Speightstown, Barbados's second main town, on the leeward side of the island. The coast here is washed by the placid waters of the Caribbean and is the "Riviera" of Barbados. The tranquil shoreline contrasts sharply with the wilder, more rugged windward coast. Relatively uncluttered with resorts, because wealthy Americans, Canadians, and Englishmen prefer to have it that way, it contains, nevertheless, a wide variety of hotels and inns ranging from the very modest to the downright luxurious. We are on Barbados's celebrated platinum coast, with the center in St. James. One of the oldest churches in the West Indies, built in 1684, is here, and an obelisk that marks the spot where Captain Powell set foot in 1625.

Barbados has a ring of beaches whose pink-white sands can be compared for softness with that of granulated sugar. East coast or west coast, the swimming is hard to beat. If you like to ride the breakers, try them on the windward Atlantic Coast.

On the west coast, Freshwater Bay, with its Paradise Beach, in the Parish of St. Michael, is aptly named. Curious "springs" appear in the sand, where underground reservoirs of fresh sheet water pressing against sea water cause the fresh water to rise to the surface.

Hence, Freshwater Bay. Ruins of one of Barbados's old forts stand at the far end of the beach. Silver Sands is south of Seawell Airport in Christ Church Parish. The early Arawaks enjoyed bathing here. Silver sand dunes and a blue surf make this colorful beach an ideal picnic-and-bathing area. Crane Beach, the site of a hotel that is a favorite with Barbadians, is just four miles north of Seawell Airport. If you prefer to brave a turbulent but safe surf, these beach waters are for you.

Another lovely beach south of Crane is Foul Bay, while northward, toward Sam Lord's Castle and beyond to Edgewater Hotel and Kittredge's Bay, are found still more lovely beaches and isolated coves, some of which are planted with coconut trees. The largest of these is Long Bay, which is outstanding because of the surrounding cliffs.

On the west coast, north of Bridgetown, the Coral Reef Club, Sandy Lane, Paradise Beach, Miramar, Colony, Buccaneer Bay Apartment Hotel, Sattler's Beach, Coconut Creek, Greensleeve Apartel, Sunset Lodge, and Eastry House are superb resorts, with beaches whose waters are more tranquil than those on the east coast of Barbados. To the south are the St. Lawrence Hotel, the Caribbee, the Royal Caribbean, the Royal-on-Sea, the lively Blue Waters Beach Hotel and Rockley Beach, the Windsor, Ocean View, Bonnie Dundee, Island Inn, Half Moon, Accra Beach, and South Winds, to name some of the best.

Inland, the stately Marine Hotel, with its magnificent swimming pool and gardens, is noted for its excellent Continental cuisine. It's the oldest hotel on the island, dating back to 1878.

On Needham's Point the new Barbados Hilton Hotel (with 150 rooms) overlooks Carlisle Bay. A new resort area has been started on the north end of the island with the North Point Surf Resort, which includes the largest swimming pool on Barbados. It is of Olympic size and contains half a million gallons of water.

Sailing is a favorite pastime, and since Barbados is, after all, an English island, horseback riding goes on everywhere.

Golf is played at a nine-hole course at Rockley Golf Club, three miles from Bridgetown, and at Sandy Lane (St. James). There are also four great spectator sports — cricket, horse racing, soccer, and polo. Race meets are held in the spring, summer, and fall on the Garrison Savannah near Bridgetown.

On November 30, 1966, the people of Barbados assumed responsibility for their own destiny. After a constitutional conference in London in June 1966, the island became independent, having its own democratic government and its own flag, national anthem, and coat of arms.

Barbados had enjoyed one of the oldest constitutional and representative systems in the Commonwealth. Its House of Assembly dates back to 1639, and the creation of an Executive Committee in 1881 was the beginning of ministerial government, which was completed by 1954. The party system was introduced in 1946, and complete internal self-government came in October 1961. One step further, independence, brought to Barbados the full right to conduct its own international affairs as an independent nation within the British Commonwealth.

ST. VINCENT

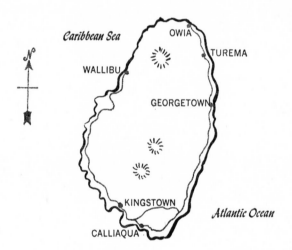

In a Nutshell:

Beautiful volcanic island, 18 miles long, 11 miles wide. Palm-lined beaches, good roads. Golf, tennis, croquet. Kingstown is the capital. Good accommodations. Airline connections with neighboring islands. Language: English. Population: 88,000.

The closest thing to a Polynesian Eden in the Caribbean is the island of St. Vincent. The fierce Carib Indians who were here when Columbus discovered the island on St. Vincent's Day in 1498 fought fiercely to keep this paradise for themselves. In the long run, Carib resistance was in vain and British obstinacy won out, long after the French had given up on St. Vincent. In addition to English and French descendant nationalities on the island, one will find Portuguese, East Indians, and Black Caribs. The latter are a result of the mingling of imported African slaves and the Indians – a fascinating polyglot population, with which only Trinidad compares.

St. Vincent is the most cheerful and possibly the gayest of the Windward Islands. On the whole, it appears to be more English than either Grenada or St. Lucia, although the gallic influence is found in such names as Chateaublair, Grand Bonhomme, and Soufrière.

The capital is Kingstown. Its red-roofed houses stand out against the green hills that form a background to the city. The main sight here is Kingstown's Botanical Gardens with its famous breadfruit tree, grown from a seed that Captain Bligh of the mutinous *Bounty* brought here from Tahiti. The colorful market place and waterfront are filled with the most engaging and happy people. There is an excellent deep-water harbor.

Besides producing its quota of sugar, coconuts, cotton, and bananas, St. Vincent is famous for growing arrowroot, a highly digestible starch utilized in food prepared for infants and invalids. Millions of tons of arrowroot are exported every year to the United States, which gives St. Vincent practically a monopoly in this field.

The countryside is magnificent from every point of view. The view from Fort Charlotte, 600 feet above Kingstown and the sea, is particularly engaging. The island's chief attraction is its volcano, called Soufrière, a name that crops up time and time again in the West Indies. This volcano erupted a day before Mont Pelée in Martinique and killed 2,000 people. This occasion never received its just attention, because of the larger catastrophe on that French-owned island. The volcano is quiet now and has a lovely crater lake.

BEQUIA (GRENADINES)

In a Nutshell:

Small island, 9 miles south of St. Vincent, part of the St. Vincent Grenadines, fine accommodations, good anchorage. Population: 3,000. Language: English.

A government schooner leaves Kingstown (St. Vincent) twice a week for the Grenadines, which lie just south of St. Vincent. The Grenadines are like a scattering of seed pearls on the velvety flow of the Caribbean. Bequia, one of the loveliest, has magnificent beaches.

Port Elizabeth is the main settlement of the little island. There are several good inns and guest houses, and two hotels: Sunny Caribbee, close to Port Elizabeth on Admiralty Bay, and Friendship Bay Hotel, just two miles away.

Princess Margaret visited the island (one of the finest beaches is named after her), and it was the winter home of Lord Avon (Anthony Eden) before he moved to Barbados. For tourists who want to escape the cares of civilization, the Grenadines are as far off the beaten path as one would care to get.

GRENADA

In a Nutshell:

The "Spice Island of the West" (some spices form the main industry). Size: 120 square miles. Beautiful mountain scenery. Picturesque capital: St. George's. Good beaches excellent hotel accommodations. Good airline connections with North and South America and the other Caribbean islands. Golf, tennis, fishing, yachtclub facilities. Language: English. Population: 87,000.

A Caribbean island that seems to have stepped out of a dream is Grenada – one of the loveliest of the very beautiful West Indian islands. For the visitor who has a feeling for rugged volcanic mountains, green tropical valleys, beautiful beaches, and an atmosphere of lazy, leisurely living, Grenada fills the bill to perfection.

Grenada is also known as the "Spice Island of the West," for cinnamon, vanilla, ginger, mayberry, and nutmeg grow here in abundance, filling the air with aromatic fragrance.

The island's greatest attraction, however, is the port of St. George's easily the most entrancing little city in the Caribbean. Houses and commercial buildings are painted in pastel hues of pink, orange, lavender, and white, creating a fanciful European village which in miniature might have come out of a Nuremberg toymaker's workshop. Only Willemstad in Curaçao and Bridgetown in Barbados might compare with St. George's, but the latter has the advantage of being smaller and therefore quainter.

A tour of the island should include lovely Grand

Anse Beach, with its fine hotels, a two-mile beach of shining sands, reputed to be one of the most beautiful in the world. In the crater of an extinct volcano is Grand Etang Lake, 1,800 feet above sea level, whose blue waters are as clear and placid as a mirror. Annandale Falls are the cascades of a mountain stream surrounded by luxuriant tropical vegetation, an idyllic spot for picnicking. The colorful market towns of Grenville and Gouyave, the second and third largest towns in Grenada, respectively, are *musts* on any tour of the island, as are the beaches at Pointe Saline and Levera Beach. The waters surrounding Levera Beach are ideal for spear fishing. Of historic as well as scenic importance is the town off Sauteurs. Here, the aboriginal Indians threw themselves into the sea rather than submit to capture by the French.

Every year brings fresh evidence of greater tourist interest in Grenada which, when one considers all the natural attractions of this island in the sun, is not surprising.

TRINIDAD

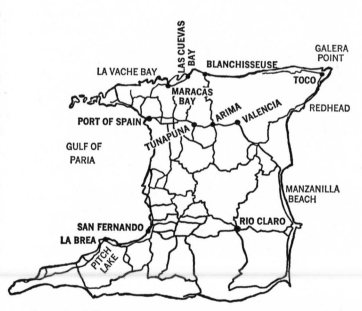

In a Nutshell:

Large island (1,882 square miles) populated with different races (East Indians, Chinese, African, English, French, Spanish, Dutch, etc.) practicing many religions. Mountains, fine beaches, good hotel accommodations. Excellent airline connections with North and South America, Europe, and other Caribbean islands. Golf, sailing (yacht club), tennis, fishing (tarpon, mackerel, red snapper), horse racing, cricket, hockey. Nightclubs. Languages: English, Spanish, and French. Population: 1,050,000.

Southernmost of the romantic Caribbean Islands, Trinidad is within sight of the South American mainland. Seen from the sea, the island is dominated by the Trinity Hills, for which Columbus named the island La Trinidad. Trinidad's topography ranges from lagoons and beaches at sea level to mountain peaks 3,000 feet high. Nature runs rampant on this island, covering the mountainsides with dense forest foliage, filling the valleys with an assortment of greenery and tropical blooms – wild orchids, bougainvillea, hibiscus, flame vine – and blessing the plains with a fertile soil where sugar cane, citrus, cocoa, and coconut plantations prosper.

"East is east and west is west, and never the twain shall meet," cried Kipling in one of his poems. Trinidad refutes this cliché in the most definite terms. For here, the most polyglot mixture of peoples east of Suez are gathered in complete harmony, living tranquilly under their own form of government and working cooperatively toward a happier and more secure future.

Port-of-Spain, the island's capital, has been called a "rendezvous of races." As you walk down the main artery of Frederick Street, you are likely to rub elbows with half the races of the world – Chinese, Japanese, East Indians, Bengalese, Syrians, Lebanese, English, French, Americans, Spanish, Dutch, Portuguese, and more.

Port-of-Spain! The capital's name puts one in mind of buccaneers, Spanish galleons, and conquistadores. Actually, it is a modern cosmopolitan center where twentieth century architecture lies cheek-by-jowl with Victorian fantasies, Hindu temples, Moslem mosques, Jewish synagogues, and Benedictine monasteries.

This wonderful diversity of peoples and places has enriched the national life of Trinidad far beyond the capacities of other islands. In this connection, one should examine the phenomenon of the steel band, which is native to Trinidad. As a musical manifestation of the island's singular variety of cultures, the steel band could only have originated in a land composed of many racial and national differences.

Although the basic drum rhythm is African, the beat and music of steel-band music is tempered by Western and Orient rhythms and East Indian dance themes.

The first recorded use of a steel container as a musical instrument dates back to 1945. A group of musicians were beating their bamboo drums when one of the drums suddenly burst. To fill the resulting gap in the rhythm, one of the players struck the empty gas tank of an abandoned car. The sound was so gratifying that players soon took to substituting anything metallic they could lay their hands on for the bamboo drums that too often burst apart – old pots, pans, garbage cans, biscuit containers, and eventually, through trial and error, the full-sized 44-gallon oil drums now in use in most developed steel bands. Steel-band players (now found in many places throughout the world) play with all the concentration of concert artists, and there is considerable merit in the claim that these players have evolved a new tonal scale. In any case, it could only have started in Trinidad.

To use an Anglican expression, "it is meet and right" that Trinidad be given the uncontested title of Calypso Capital of the World. Developed out of the folk songs and folk music of the Afro-West Indian, calypso is warm and moving as music, and its lyrics command close attention. Witty, rich in innuendo and satire, calypso is the creation of a poet-musician who composes both lyrics and music. He is in a sense the mouthpiece of his people, revealing their feelings and opinions, sufferings and aspirations, fears and bravado on an extremely wide range of subjects – local and foreign, social, political, economic, personal. He is this century's answer to the town crier, the village gossip, the jungle telegraph, a highly vocal version of Paris' Daumier and the moving spirit of a whole new world of music. Calypso, holding the mirror up to nature, is much more than rich entertainment – when its history is finally written, calypso will be ranked as a permanent record of life and thought in Trinidad and Tobago.

Almost all of Trinidad's superb beaches are accessible by roads, and in the northern, mountainous region of the island, the views are spectacular enough to warrant day-long tours – even without dipping a toe in the fantastically lucid waters. The Saddle Road, winding through Maraval Valley, climbs upward to the Skyline Highway, from there to marvelous Maracas Beach, with its charming al fresco restaurant under a canopy of palms, and on to Las Cuevas Beach. Toco Beach, on the northeast "corner" of Trinidad, exhausts one's supply of superlatives in describing its natural beauty.

In Port-of-Spain, the capital, are found some remarkable edifices: mosques, estate houses, and private homes on the Savannah – 200 acres that form the *mis en scène* for the unbelievable carnivals. Nearby is St. Andrew's Golf Club, founded in 1890 by a few homesick Scottish exiles and moved in 1935 to its present home in Maraval.

Just around the corner is Trinidad's famous Country Club, the hub of the colonists' social universe. Once a private home, now owned by T. B. Fernandes (rum distillers), the club sprawls on six lovely acres studded with cypresses, butterfruit trees, samaans, and other rare trees. There is a huge swimming pool, ten tennis courts, a ballroom, restaurant, bars, and ivy-clad outbuildings, all for the pleasure of the 4,000 members. Cricket, a passionate favorite with Trinidadians, is played in Queen's Park Oval, which can hold 30,000 spectators; all roads leading to the Oval are crammed with motor cars during an important match.

Once upon a time a tribe of mighty Carib Indian warriors inhabited a tropic island of great beauty known today as Trinidad. To celebrate the defeat of its enemies, one of the tribesmen shot and killed the hummingbird, sacred to the gods. The wrathful great spirits in punishment caused their entire village to disappear into the depths of the earth, and in its place arose a dark and mysterious lake.

Thus goes the legend of Trinidad's famous Pitch Lake. In actuality, this lake came into existence millions of years ago, when large quantities of asphaltic oil seeped into a mud volcano. The volcano churned the oil, mixing it with gases and great pressure, until the oil was converted into asphalt. The lighter portions of this substance have evaporated over the course of years, and the residue forms Trinidad's world-famous Asphalt Lake of today.

The earliest record of this strange substance is found in the diary of Sir Walter Raleigh, who discovered Pitch Lake in 1595. He wrote: "There is an abundance of stone pitch. All the ships of the world may be therewith ladened from thence. We made trial in trimming our ships and found it to be most excellent good; it melteth not with the sun as doth the pitch from Norway and for ships trading the south parts it is very good." Raleigh used a good deal of pitch from this lake to calk his boats, and it is still used as marine glue today.

In 1792, machinery was set up to refine the pitch and extract its oil for burning in lamps. For years a profitable trade was carried on with the motherland, Spain.

You can walk on this lake, because the asphalt is hard, so hard that it must be dug with pick axes. Wherever you dig one day, the hole is completely filled the next day. Thus Pitch Lake continuously replenishes itself.

It covers about 100 acres in a large circular depression. Nearly 300 feet deep in the middle, the whole mass is in a constant state of movement because of the evolution of gas in the center and the continuous influx of new material into the lake.

Trinidad is proud of its Pitch Lake. Its virtually inexhaustible supply of asphalt covers the highways of the world, protects buildings from damp, and serves daily needs in many ways. Today, when you walk the streets of London, New York, Madrid, Cadiz, or Paris, you walk on a part of Trinidad, for all these streets are paved with the famous pitch that Sir Walter Raleigh found "most excellent good."

When Columbus discovered Trinidad on his third voyage to the New World, he found an Amerindian people, friendly but suspicious. They were of the Arawak tribe, a peaceful people by comparison with the warlike Caribs who raided the territory from the South American mainland with dependable regularity. Columbus noted that the Arawaks were a graceful and handsome people who wore their dark hair cut in a style similar to the Spanish mode of the day and who dressed with gaily colored head scarves and a minimum of clothing. They lived in settled villages, cultivated small crops, expressed their artistry in pottery and basketry. The Amerindian was polytheistic, loved dancing, produced music with drums and conch shells, and played a primitive type of competitive ball game. Along with his tobacco, cassava, decorative pottery, and highly efficient, seaworthy pirogue, he bequeathed to us many fascinating place names: Chacachacare and Guayaguayare, Tamana and Cumuto, Arima, Naparima, Tunapuna, Caroni and Carapichaima, and others.

Although any purity of native Amerindian blood has long ceased to exist, the strain has its place in the indigenous population, and many are proud of their "Carib" heritage, celebrated annually in the town of Arima with the Feast of Santa Rosa.

Before leaving Trinidad, a word should be said about the magnificent Mardi Gras Carnival staged here. Carnival connoisseurs the world over are unanimous in proclaiming Trinidad's pre-Lenten festival the wildest, gaudiest, most exhilarating, most exhausting, most pictorially gratifying Carnival anywhere.

Officially lasting only three days – until Ash Wednesday – Carnival actually begins weeks before in the feverish preparation of costumes, exquisite or outlandish; masks, headdress ornaments, mechanically activated accouterments; special effects such as fireworks, sputtering rockets, and the like. Some costumes mount into the hundreds of BWI dollars, some fly into the thousands. Competing bands number their members and instrumentalists from a modest few to as many as 1,000 members, everyone competing at every level with gay ferocity.

Rumblings and bangings, melodies and cacophonies are ear-splitting in the back alleys of Port-of-Spain as early as Thursday, when prudent shopkeepers begin boarding up store fronts. Accompanying the general noise of the practicing tamboo-bamboo and steel bands is the irreverent vocalizing of the kaiso singers. "Kaiso" goes back to the nickname of a *chantuelle*, the slave-troubadour of a wealthy sixteenth-century French immigrant. In whatever way "kaiso" became corrupted into "calypso" is no matter – what matters is that the tradition of kaiso has remained alive through the centuries.

TOBAGO

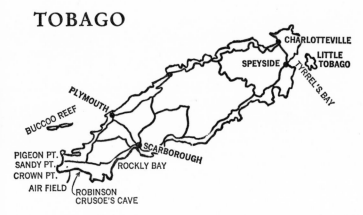

In a Nutshell:

Interesting mountain island (116 square miles), exotic birds, beautiful tropical vegetation. Close to Trinidad. 26 miles long, 7½ miles wide. Capital: Scarborough. Skin diving and fishing rewarding. Excellent hotel accommodations. Good airline connections with North America and other Caribbeans islands. Language: English. Population: 35,000.

Tobagonians, as the inhabitants of Tobago are called, believe that Daniel Defoe had their island in mind when he described the adventures of Robinson Crusoe. Although this point might be debated, there is no arguing the fact that Tobago presents an idyllic tropical setting.

Situated twenty miles northeast of Trinidad, Tobago is a mountainous island of fertile valleys, plenty of tropical vegetation, indescribably beautiful virgin beaches, and an atmosphere of peace and quiet that is highly recommended to the tense citizens of more northerly climes.

Rum and sugar helped to make fortunes in Tobago in colonial days, a fact that was not overlooked by the British, French, Spanish, and Dutch, who fought for her and took possession at one time or another. Although the English finally won out, Tobago and Trinidad have emerged in recent years from their colonial status as completely independent members of the British Commonwealth of Nations.

One can visit Tobago either by plane or by booking passage on regularly scheduled coastal steamers leaving Trinidad. The trip by boat takes two hours and is a pleasant cruise. Scarborough, the capital, will be your landing place. It is easily the quietest little colonial village under the sun, although on market days the town offers a somewhat more active atmosphere. A drive or walk to Old Fort George is recommended. From its hilltop location, you will see one of the more magnificent Caribbean seascapes.

One of Tobago's show places, Buccoo Reef, is off the western end of the island, near Pigeon Point. Buccoo Reef is proud of its nearby Nylon Pool of sparkling aquamarine water, perhaps the clearest, most transparent water in the entire Caribbean. Glass-bottom boats take visitors to the reef, a favorite meeting place for snorkelers who delight in the crystal-clear waters and interesting sea gardens.

Well worth a visit is Arnos Vale, on the northwestern coast of Tobago. Distant reefs enclose and protect the small bay and resort, giving it very calm, deep-blue waters, a paradise for snorkeling, with a unique and magnificent sea garden.

Little Tobago, just off the northeastern tip of Tobago, is a well-known bird sanctuary. Famous for the lovely birds of paradise that nest here, the sanctuary was started in 1909, when the owner of Little Tobago brought 26 pairs of this colorful bird to the island. After his death in 1929, his sons gave the island to the Trinidad-Tobago government, with the provision that it be used as a bird sanctuary.

THE NETHERLANDS ANTILLES

Most of the islands of the Caribbean received their culture and development from such great European powers as England, France, and Spain. There is, however, a group of islands—or rather, two groups, if we are to speak geographically – that come under the sphere of influence of a fourth major European colonial power—Holland. If you can imagine such cities as Delft, the Hague, and Edam transferred to the tropics, you can picture the charm of the Netherlands Antilles. The cleanliness of Dutch streets, the typical Dutch architecture of their many-gabled homes, and the marvelous creative energy of the people are part and parcel of the wonderful charm of such islands as Aruba, Bonaire, Curaçao, St. Martin, St. Eustatius, and Saba. (We have already discussed St. Martin and Saba.)

Curaçao, the island that nobody wanted (at first), was discovered by Amerigo Vespucci in 1499 and settled (by the Spanish) in 1527. In 1634 the powerful Netherlands West Indian Company arrived and displaced the Spanish colony. Nine years later, the redoubtable Peter Stuyvesant was appointed governor of Curaçao. While leading an expedition against Sint Maarten a year later, he was wounded in the leg. The limb was amputated and buried in Curaçao. Except for a brief period of English occupation and control during the Napoleonic wars, the island has remained under the Dutch flag for more than three hundred years.

CURAÇAO

In a Nutshell:

Largest of the Netherlands Antilles (173 square miles). Has one of the busiest ports in the world. Capital: Willemstad, a rich commercial city. Main industry – oil refineries. Golf, fishing, sailing. Famous free port. Excellent hotel accommodations. Airline connections with North and South America, Europe, and the other West Indian islands. Languages: Dutch, English, Spanish, and Papiamento. Population: 136,000.

Prosperous Curaçao is one of those rare Caribbean islands whose standard of living is comparable to that of the more highly developed countries of North America. It is the largest of the six islands comprising the Netherlands Antilles. It is perhaps the most cosmopolitan and commercial island in the Caribbean.

Curaçao's financial success is due to its status as an international shopping center, its excellent port facilities, and its great oil refineries. The latter industry, in particular, was the great boost that lifted Curaçao out of its nineteenth-century economic doldrums. With the discovery of oil in Venezuela's Lake Maracaibo and the installation of one of the world's biggest oil refineries in Curaçao, great prosperity came to this little Dutch island. As they say here, when the wind blows from the refineries, the air smells of money.

Naturally, this prosperous island has attracted people from far and wide, and not from the Caribbean alone. Americans, Dutch, Spanish, Portuguese, Hindus, West and East Indians, Chinese, Javanese, and Venezuelans are all part of the melting pot that forms the basic population of twentieth-century Curaçao.

As colorful as the people is the capital, Willemstad. It is distinctively Dutch – and European. Gabled houses of seventeenth-century Dutch architecture are painted with a full palette of ice-cream-soda colors: lime, strawberry, chocolate, pistachio, and vanilla, with a sprinkling of yellow, red, and lilac.

Willemstad is divided into two main sections, separated by the deep channel of St. Anna Bay and tied together by the most famous bridge in the Caribbean. This is the world-renowned Queen Emma Bridge – a hinged pontoon affair that seems to breathe. Walking across it, you can feel it move up and down beneath you. Visitors never seem to tire of watching the bridge swing open and fold itself against the quay to let ocean liners and freighters enter or depart the port.

The finest shopping center in the Caribbean is found in the Punda Section of Willemstad. Smart shops like Spritzer and Fuhrmann, El Globo, van Dorp, and others maintain an incredible stock of the world's finest merchandise. Prices are low because Curaçao is practically a free port.

Curaçao has a special attraction for linguists. It is here that the first new language in hundreds of years has been created. It is called Papiamento. Spoken by everyone, it is fast becoming a written language, as well. One writer has described Papiamento as a linguistic cocktail — three ounces of Spanish, one ounce of Dutch, one-half ounce of English, French, and African, and a dash of Portuguese. Papiamento is most readily understood by Dutch- and Spanish-speaking peoples.

Curaçao boasts few good beaches, and there are none at all in Willemstad, which, on the other hand, does have an oversize swimming pool at the unique Curaçao Intercontinental Hotel and a somewhat smaller one at the Hotel Avila.

Sights to see in the capital should include three interesting statues. Peter Stuyvesant, who lost his leg in an attack on Sint Maarten, is represented in bronze. Simón Bolívar, who was effective in establishing friendly relations between Venezuela and Curaçao, is prominently represented. The most impressive statue, however, is that of Queen Wilhelmina, under whose rule Curaçao came to economic prominence in the Caribbean.

In Willemstad one should also take in the lovely Dutch Reformed Church built in 1769 and the Mikve Israel Synagogue (1732). The latter building is an outstanding example of eighteenth-century Dutch architecture. Seven miles from town is Hato Airport, a tourist sight in itself and one of the world's great terminals.

Outside Willemstad, the countryside has a charm all its own. Here you will see cactus plants growing twenty feet high — and the weird divi-divi trees. These grow to a height of ten feet and then thrust out trunk and branches at a right angle from the lower trunk for another ten feet or more; they appear to be growing sideways, with the trade winds, rather than vertically.

Generally the countryside is dry. In picturesque thatched huts and adobe homes you will see families weaving straw and pounding meal, and on the coast the native fishermen cast their nets. Occasionally, a handsome colonial estate, or *landhuis*, emerges, inviting you to investigate its attractions.

A guided tour will take you all the way to the northwestern tip and along the north coast. En route you will want to see the Boca Tabla, a grotto carved out by the sea. There are excellent beaches on the leeward (southwestern) coast at Knip Bay, Piscadera Bay, Spanish Water, Santa Marta, Santa Cruz, and Westpoint; the last-named is a twenty-five-mile drive from Willemstad. Here, too, are the remains of an old stone settlement, a fishing village, and the bluest water imaginable.

Before the erection of the Hotel Curaçao Intercontinental, accommodations in Willemstad were so limited that few tourists remained here more than a day or so. The advent of this luxurious hotel in the Intercontinental chain in 1957 changed tourist habits in Curaçao. Built right into the old seaside fort that was constructed by the Dutch in 1827 — the massive walls are thirty-three feet thick — the Curaçao Intercontinental is a happy blend of site and architecture. The ramparts of the fort now serve as a promenade for guests. They form an arc, partly facing the open sea, whose surf pounds at the base of the fort, and partly facing the narrow channel leading to the harbor. Boats pass so close that guests can easily exchange remarks with the officers and crew.

The success of the Intercontinental inspired the building of more hostelries. The Curaçao Hilton (1967), with 200 ultramodern guest rooms, is situated on a beautiful beach on Piscadera Bay. There is also a luxurious gambling casino, glass-enclosed outside elevators, excellent convention facilities, restaurants, bars, shops, a swimming pool, a ballroom, and all the comforts for which Hilton is famous.

The Flamboyant Beach Hotel (1967), on the south coast near Willemstad, has a fine beach, seventy-two ocean-front rooms, a huge swimming pool and cabana club, and other modern facilities.

The Coral Cliff Hotel, on a secluded beach on Santa Marta Bay, twenty-four miles northwest of Willemstad, has thirty-five air-conditioned rooms, all with balconies overlooking the bay. There is a marina, an observatory, deep-sea fishing, water skiing, snorkeling, sailing, tennis, and much more.

The Country Inn, a motel with seventy-two cozy, air-conditioned rooms with kitchenette, refrigerator, television, and radio, is near Willemstad. There is a swimming pool, cafeteria, self-service barbecue, tennis, volleyball, midget golf, *bolas criollas,* and a children's playground on the premises.

A Holiday Inn (1968) with two hundred rooms is elegant and comfortable. Also the older hotels are modernized and offer a lot to the tourist.

The Avila Beach Hotel is a former governor's palace, with thirty-eight air-conditioned rooms, a romantic restaurant, a schooner bar, and beautiful gardens directly on a private beach.

The Piscadera Bay Club is a resort-type hotel on spacious grounds with a beautiful private beach on Piscadera Bay near Willemstad (forty-five air-conditioned rooms). Next door is the Curaçao Hilton.

BONAIRE

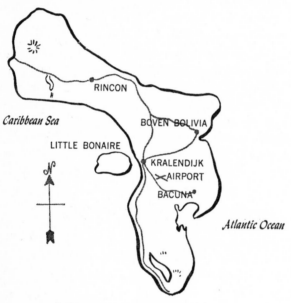

In a Nutshell:

Off the beaten path, but close to Curaçao. Size: 112 square miles. Especially interesting for its birdlife. The large flamingo colony is world-famous — and there are many varieties of parrots, parakeets, herons, terns, snipes. Beautiful submarine life, deep-sea and spearfishing. Capital: Kralendijk. Good accommodations. Excellent airline connections with Curaçao. Languages: Dutch and English. Population: 7,500.

Bonaire is a unique island in the sun. Lying close to the Venezuelan coast — only twenty minutes by air from Curaçao — the island's centuries-old rustic charms and tranquillity blend with modern improvements, up-to-date roads, and good hotel accommodations to provide a constant lure for holiday seekers and nature lovers.

Bonaire is virgin territory of almost unbelievable loveliness for tourists, honeymooners, skin divers, bird fanciers, photographers, and everyone seeking escape from the tensions of the workaday world.

The capital, Kralendijk (Coral Dike), is as Dutch as its name. Painted in orange, pink, and green, with neat gardens, a Lilliputian harbor, pink fish market, and midget boats, this toy capital is ideal for sightseeing.

A trip through the countryside will take you to beautiful plantations, the great salt lakes, and the northern hill country, which looks like a midget edition of the "wild West." If you like picnicking, sail over to Little Bonaire, a tiny, uninhabited island only three miles square.

For some reason known only to Mother Nature, Bonaire was selected as the mating and breeding place for thousands of pink flamingos. The sight of these colorful birds sitting on their pie-shaped nests and tending their young attracts bird lovers by the hundreds year after year. The island is also a showcase of thousands of herons, snipe, terns, pelicans, green parrots, parakeets, warbirds, and other tropical species of brilliant plumage.

In Bonaire, lovely white-sand beaches abound, and the crystal-clear waters are a year-round attraction to skin divers, spearfishermen, and water skiers.

The waters that surround Bonaire constitute a fisherman's paradise. Sea bass, kingfish, sailfish, bonito, barracuda, snapper, perch, grouper, pompano, and a myriad of rainbow-hued fishes fairly teem in these waters. Sea crayfish and spinal lobster can be speared in shallow waters along the coast.

Bonaire is an island designed for nature lovers who long for a really different vacation. There is no hustle, no bustle, and no frantic search for diversion. It is just a hideaway world relaxation and fun, bathed in the constant breezes of the Trade Winds, a little island of peace and pleasure in the Caribbean.

ARUBA

In a Nutshell:

Dutch island, 18 miles from coast of Venezuela. Ideal place for vacationing, relaxing. Magnificent beaches, dry, healthy climate cooled by trade winds, almost no rainfall. Excellent hotel accomodations. Size: 70 square miles. Capital: Oranjestad. A free port with excellent shops. Gambling casino, golf, yacht club, tennis, horseback riding, water

skiing, fishing. Direct airline connections with North and South America, Europe, and the other Caribbean islands. Languages: Dutch, English, Spanish, and Papiamento. Population: 60,000.

If the Cinderalla story were to be applied to islands, Aruba would qualify for the leading role. In little more than thirty years, Aruba has changed from a sleepy, neglected, deserted, almost barren little island into a bustling, thriving, tourist-attracting area.

So little impression did Aruba make on colonial explorers and exploiters that its native Indian population was left singularly in peace, and until the Indians were more or less absorbed by the early settlers, the island was a sort of unofficial reservation for the Indians. It is believed that almost two thirds of the population on the island are of part-Indian descent.

Oranjestad is the capital. A more civilized little city would be hard to find. It is Dutch-clean, which is to say immaculate. Narrow houses reveal the Dutch influence in their red-gabled roofs. Neat gardens bloom with a pink-and-white flower called *bruidstranen*, or "bride's tears," and *mannenkarakter*, a pink-and-white vine. Even the port area of Oranjestad is a shining example of cleanliness, all the more striking when one considers that 500 ships load and discharge their goods here annually. The market place near the quay displays colorful tropical fruits and vegetables in an area that is almost supermarket neat. Vegetables here are not earth-grown but are cultivated in air and water in great vegetable nurseries, which are well worth visiting. Small rainfall, with a resulting shortage of water, has required the construction of water distilleries to supply the population with its basic liquid requirements.

Aruba's natural attractions do not include those marvels that constitute the magnificence of many Caribbean islands – volcanic peaks, rain forests, lush tropical vegetation. Aruba has none of these – but it does have some of the most beautiful beaches in the Caribbean, a dry, healthful climate, and a landscape that is truly picturesque. The giant cactus, the golden *kibracha* or break-ax tree with its profusion of yellow blooms, and the exotic divi-divi tree with its branches blown to the west by the prevailing trade winds are fascinating growths.

Aruba looks to the visitor to its southwestern resort coast almost like an unending beach of snow-white sand. It is an ideal location for rest and relaxation, with nightclubs, casinos, luxurious hotels, excellent restaurants, always good weather – a dream vacation land. But there is more than all this to Aruba, one of the leading resort islands of the Caribbean.

On the southeast end of Aruba, far from the beaches and the capital, Oranjestad, is the largest oil refinery in the world, that of the Lago Oil & Transport Co., Ltd., between the American settlements of San Nicolas and Seroe Colorado. Thanks to this subsidiary of the Standard Oil Company of New Jersey, Aruba exports well over 360 million dollars' worth of petroleum products annually, refined from Venezuelan oil.

Aruba is duly grateful to its benefactor, but no longer exclusively beholden, because in recent years its many miles of coral-free beaches, quaint towns, fascinating native flora and fauna, and impressive landscapes and seascapes have created a rewarding tourist industry.

Today, with oil and tourism, Aruba is one of the richer Caribbean islands.

CAYMAN ISLANDS

In a Nutshell:

Three small islands of which only Grand Cayman and Cayman Brac are ready for vacationers. Beautiful beaches, a paradise for fishermen. Good accommodations and food. Airport at Georgetown on Grand Cayman. Excellent airline connections with Miami, Jamaica, and Central America and between the islands. Language: English. Population: 10,000, mostly white.

About 180 miles northwest of Jamaica are the "islands that time forgot." There are the Cayman (Alligator)

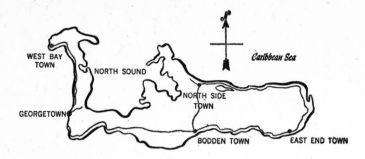

WEST BAY TOWN
NORTH SOUND
GEORGETOWN
NORTH SIDE TOWN
BODDEN TOWN
EAST END TOWN
Caribbean Sea

Islands, consisting of Grand Cayman, Little Cayman, and Cayman Brac, all of which are relatively flat as Caribbean islands go, and only one of which, Grand Cayman, has developed larger hotels and resorts. There is a fine little inn on Cayman Brac.

Ethnically speaking, Caymanians are unique in the West Indies, for the white population outnumbers the Negro here and is descended from buccaneers, ship-wrecked sailors, and Scottish farmers. Since many of the males eventually end up as sailors – Caymanians are expert seamen – there are about four times as many women as men on the islands, a fact that should not be misleading, as moral standards are exceedingly high here, as befits a strict church-going people.

Despite their British origin and connections, Caymanians tend to have a great affection for, and affinity to, the American way of life, particularly in matters that concern business and personal interests. Enlightened Caymanians prefer to go to Tampa, Florida, for example, for fun and shopping than to Mother Jamaica, a fact that is not altogether appreciated on the Big Island.

The Cayman Islands are famous for the diversity of tropical vegetation. Grand Cayman, particularly, blazes with flowering trees and bougainvillea. Colorful birds adorn vines and trees, adding luster to the tropical scene. Relatively unspoiled, Grand Cayman, Little Cayman, and Cayman Brac are still sufficiently off the beaten path to be an ideal retreat for the holiday seeker who wants complete relaxation.

The islands offer wonderful facilities for swimming off beaches whose real-estate value has increased a thousandfold in recent years. Sailing, snorkeling, spear-fishing, deep-sea fishing, lobster progging, and wild-duck hunting are favorite activities with sportsmen. In colonial days, the Cayman Islands were notorious as pirate lairs. Today, buried treasure is still unearthed by a fortunate and persistent few.

THE PLATES

1 Jamaica: Calypso Group (Montego Bay)

Calypso entertainment wherever you go: the beach, at the hotels, in the night clubs – and you know you're in Jamaica! In Jamaica, the music of calypso melodies is everywhere. The gaiety in the air makes this island the liveliest in the Caribbean. Calypso, a form of folk music and song, originated and developed in the Caribbean, especially in Jamaica.

2 Jamaica: Port Antonio

This is Jamaica: high mountains, deep-green, lush vegetation, beautiful harbors, palm-framed beaches, friendly villages and, all around, the clear, blue water of the Caribbean Sea. The photograph depicts one of the loveliest areas of Jamaica, a part of the northeast coast. Here, Nature has been at her most lavish, and beautiful vistas abound. The views shows the twin harbors of Port Antonio, with the town proper on the distant promontory and, on the nearer point, the Folly lighthouse.

3 Jamaica: A Beach on the North Shore (Ocho Rios)

Typical of the island's beautiful beaches is this one on the north coast. Framed by the ever-present coconut palms, with the mountains always in the background, the shore of white sand meets the blue Caribbean to form a pleasure spot for swimming, sailing, and quiet relaxation in the sun. Like Montego Bay, the midnorth shore region of Ocho Rios is a holiday center with excellent modern hotels and full facilities for vacation fun.

4 Jamaica: Ruins at Discovery Bay

Columbus landed at this bay in 1494. Not far from here was the first Spanish settlement of Sevilla Nueva, founded in 1509. Only a few ruins remain.

5 Haiti: The Magnificent Waterfalls of Saut d'Eau

Haitians celebrate St. Mary's Day at Haiti's highest waterfall, the famed Saut d'Eau, by cleansing themselves in symbolic purification beneath the falling waters. Strange Voodoo overtones are involved in this ritual. Nothing in Haiti is more fascinating than the living practice of Voodoo, a pagan African religion mixed with Christian belief.

6 Haiti: Ruins of Sans Souci Palace at Milot

The present ruins of this "Versailles of the New World" which Henri Christophe built more than a century and a half ago inspire the imagination to recreate the magnificence that once was the Palace of Sans Souci. In this connection one must visit also the most monumental structure in the West Indies, if not the Western World – the Citadelle nearby. Built by the hand labor of 200,000 ex-slaves, it is a masterpiece of architectural engineering and an awesome reminder of Haiti's turbulent history.

7 Dominican Republic: Ruins of Monastery of St. Francis, Santo Domingo

Magnificent flowers and tropical vegetation grow in the well-kept gardens adjoining the ancient stone walls of this relic of Columbus's day, of which only the arches and towers remain. Other historic sites are the Cathedral of Santa Maria la Menor, where the Admiral's bones are buried, and the Alcázar, fortress home of Diego Columbus, the Discoverer's son.

8 Dominican Republic: Modern Santo Domingo

The capital of the Dominican Republic gleams in the background across blue Caribbean waters and a rock-bound coastline. The city is bright with magnificent boulevards and lovely parks and botanical gardens. Some of the finest hotels in the Caribbean are here.

9 Puerto Rico: The Fortaleza, Governor's Residence in San Juan

The official residence of the Governor of Puerto Rico is open to the public and is well worth visiting. The edifice dates back to 1533, when it was a fort. Burned by the Dutch, rebuilt in 1640, and restored in 1847, it is the oldest executive mansion in the Western hemisphere in use. The Fortaleza has been a seat of Puerto Rico's government for more than four centuries.

10 Puerto Rico: History and Modern Life in San Juan

Just over the palm trees in the center of the photo is seen the historic fort of San Gerónimo, one of the three small forts built to protect the landward end of San Juan Island. Finished about the end of the eighteenth century, it played an important role during the English attack of 1797. It is today a museum of considerable importance in the culture of San Juan. Just beyond, we skip over a small body of water and almost two hundred years in time to modern San Juan's fabulous resorts. To the left is the San Gerónimo Hotel, to the right the Flamboyant Hotel, with La Concha and the Sheraton beyond them. The up-to-date city of San Juan is background to it all.

11 Castillo de San Felipe del Morro, San Juan, Puerto Rico

This great fortress is the chief tourist attraction of Old San Juan. Built by the Spanish at the northwest tip of the city from 1539 to 1586, it covers more than 200 acres and rises 145 feet above the Atlantic. The castle was continually improved until 1783.

Philip II of Spain, conscious of the need to fortify the Indies, commissioned General Juan de Tejeda to plan fortifications in all the important seaports of the Caribbean. Puerto Rico, being the most easterly of the islands and possessing a magnificent harbor, would become an excellent entrance to the Caribbean, the king thought, if well defended.

For the construction of the military defenses in Puerto Rico, the local royal funds, the voluntary services of the inhabitants, and funds from the treasury of Nueva España (Mexico) were used. The official design of the fortress, which came to be known as El Morro, was made by Juan Bautista Antonelli. Additions were later made by governors Pedro de Salazar, Menéndez, and Suares Coronel.

Like those in many other seaport towns of the Spanish Main, the fortress of El Morro was built on a promontory as an impregnable harbor defense. El Morro commanded the main entrance, assisted by a battery called Santa Elena, while El Morrillo and the Cabrón batteries took care of the eastern shore and the Boquerón Fort at the shore end of the island of San Juan. In 1598, the artillery numbered eighty-eight pieces in all.

12   Tortola: British Virgin Islands

The British Virgin Islands are quite different in atmosphere and history from the other (U.S.) Virgin Islands. These beautiful islands are definitely on the reserved and quiet side and are ideal for dreamers and people seeking complete relaxation.

13   Virgin Islands: A Typical View from Road Town

So peaceful, unique and unspoiled are the natural beauties and general appearance of the Virgin Islands, you are mindful of what the earth was like at its creation. The islands are easily seen to be part of a huge underwater mountain range of which only the highest peaks (about a hundred) emerge from the ocean.

14   St. Thomas Aerial Tramway

In a matter of minutes you are whisked to the top of thousand-foot-high Flag Hill on this amazing funicular. Three stops on the way up and on the way down enable you to take pictures from different heights and to enjoy still longer the beautiful outlook. There is a magnificent view of St. Thomas and the islands in the neighborhood: St. Croix, Tortola, St. John, Virgin Gorda, Vieques, Puerto Rico, and others.

15   Carnival in St. Thomas

One of the great events in the Virgin Islands is the carnival in St. Thomas. At this time the streets of Charlotte Amalie are a riot of colors, with the population in gay costumes and carnival hats. There are dancing groups, and everyone joins in the general festivities, with parades, bands, and fair. Being tourist-minded, the people of St. Thomas celebrate Carnival when their tourist

season ends, in the last week of April, to tempt visitors to prolong their stay. Friday and Saturday of this Carnival week are legal holidays by proclamation of the Governor.

16   St. Thomas (U. S. Virgin Islands): View of Charlotte Amalie

One of the great views of St. Thomas. As we look down from the terrace of Mafolie, the harbor of St. Thomas and the city of Charlotte Amalie surround us.
Charlotte Amalie is the real tourist center of the Virgin Islands. The city occupies a particularly beautiful site spread over three hills. The narrow streets, romantic restaurants, night clubs, palm-shaded patios, and luxurious free-port shops give the city great charm. Charlotte Amalie is the starting place from which most tourists begin their trips to the other Virgin Islands.

17   Christiansted, Capital of St. Croix U. S. Virgin Islands

A sight never to be forgotten: This well-preserved Danish port, for many years also capital of the Danish Virgin Islands, with its romantic streets and its interesting historic buildings painted in pastel colors, is one of the highlights of every Caribbean visit.

18   Christiansted, St. Croix: Old Danish Government House

One of the outstanding old Danish buildings in St. Croix is the Government House along King Street, built in the eighteenth century, with later additions such as this beautiful stairway and façade, finished in 1830. Formerly the residence of the Governor of the Danish West Indies, it also included the main offices of the Colonial Government. Among the highlights are the great ballroom and the old kitchen. The building reflects the wealth and importance of St. Croix in the late eighteenth and early nineteenth century as a fabulous sugar island. In 1755, about nine thousand slaves were working here in the plantations; by 1804, however, 27,349 slaves were owned by the planters. The Government House and the wharf area are a National Historic Site, preserved by the U. S. Department of the

Interior and the Government of the U. S. Virgin Islands. They are excellent examples of the old Danish economy and way of life in the Virgin Islands.

19 Fort Christianvaern (St. Croix)

Close to the harbor of Christiansted is Fort Christianvaern, built in the eighteenth century, during the island's greatest boom. The Danish West India and Guinea Company had just sold the island to the Danish King (1755), and St. Croix became the "Fabulous Sugar Island." Today, vines and flowers grow over the fortifications that used to protect the harbor.

20 St. Croix (Virgin Islands):
Ruins of a Plantation

There are many such ruins in St. Croix. It was one of the richest sugar islands, with more than 53% of its total area planted with sugar cane. In 1804, some 21,000 slaves were working on the many plantations. A rapid economic decline set in during 1820. The debts of the planters rose to 76% of their holdings; many lost their lands by mortgage foreclosures, money for improvements became scarce, and other markets such as Cuba and Puerto Rico outgrew St. Croix. Finally Denmark prohibited slave trading and in 1848 proclaimed the emancipation of all the unfree in the Danish West Indies. This was the end of St. Croix's competitive position. The laborers became embittered and many of the island's plantations were destroyed in riots. The ruins remain, appealing to romantics. Even their former names are redolent of a bygone era: Judith's Fancy, Anna's Hope, Peter's Rest, Upper Love, Jealousy, Little Princess, Betsy's Jewel, Wheel of Fortune, and many more. Vines and flowers cover the old stone walls.

21 St. John (U. S. Virgin Islands):
Romantic Caneel Bay

St. John is a beautiful island consisting of lovely beaches, mountains, lush tropical vegetation, and a great National Park. Behind all the island's beauty lies a tragic history. Less than two and a half centuries ago, there were more than a hundred rich estates and sugar cane plantations, which made it one of the most flourishing of the Virgins. In 1733 a bloody slave rebellion exterminated all the white inhabitants. Since that time, trees and jungle have grown over the destroyed plantations, and their ruins are visible under the dense forest of vegetation.

22 View overlooking Dutch Sint Maarten: Philipsburg

Philipsburg has the most unique setting for a capital city in all the West Indies. It is situated on a narrow crescent strip of land between ocean and lake. Since horseback-riding is one of the favorite island sports, it is worth while to ride the scenic trails to any of the heights above Philipsburg for a fascinating view of the city. A local legend describes how the island was divided between the French and Dutch. In 1648, a dispute over sovereignty was settled by a walking contest. A Frenchman and a Dutchman started from the same point and walked in opposite directions until they met. The Frenchman walked faster and claimed the larger portion of the island, but the Dutch half included the salt pans near Philipsburg that for a century made Sint Maarten one of the most valuable properties of the Netherlands West India Company.

23 St. Kitts (St. Christopher): Brimstone Hill,
Old British Fortification

Ten miles from Basseterre, capital of St. Kitts, is the fantastic fortress of Brimstone Hill, "The Gibraltar of the West Indies." Thousands of slaves labored for a hundred years to raise its walls, 700 feet high. It is said the Brimstone Hill Fort inspired Henri Christophe to build his Citadelle in Haiti. A view from the ramparts includes the outlying islands of Saint Eustatius, Saba, Sint Maarten, and Montserrat.

24 The Island of Saba: An Extinct Volcano

Like a tremendous rock cast into the sea, Saba emerges starkly from surrounding Caribbean waters. Three small villages are visible on the slopes and shoulders of the volcanic cone, of which the highest and smallest, close to the crater, is called Hellsgate. Clearly visible is the steep road that connects the other two villages.

These are Bottom (situated on top of the mountain) and Windwardside. Saba is one of the great showplace islands of the West Indies and can easily be reached from Sint Maarten by boat or airplane.

25 Strolling the Beach at Nevis

A great sweep of unspoiled beaches is characteristic of the coastline of Nevis, at one time the most important health resort of the West Indies. The volcanic island possesses all the wonderful advantages of Nature. Forest-clad hills rise from the sea to a height of 3,596 feet, and there are many good beaches and much interesting scenery. Columbus called the island Las Nievas – snow – comparing the white clouds that crowned the crest of the island's peaks with the snow-topped range of mountains he was familiar with in northern Spain. Nevis was the birthplace of Alexander Hamilton.

26 Antigua: Historic English Harbour

One of the spectacular attractions of Antigua is English Harbour where Lord Nelson labored to prepare his fleet, which in time destroyed Napoleon's sea-power. The pillars of the workshop at Nelson's Dockyard are still standing, as well as long lines of decaying walls, arches, and gun emplacements. As you pass through the Dockyard gates, you have the impression of being translated to the late eighteenth century; old cannons, anchors, sundials, and caldrons for boiling pitch abound. The entire area is alive with memories of Antigua's exciting and romantic past.

27 Antigua: A Typical Caribbean Scene – Ruins of a Sugar Mill

Much of Caribbean local color is contained in this scene: the old sugar mill, the native woman with basket on head, the children astride the mule, could have been photographed on almost any of the Caribbean Islands. To make the picture complete, sheaves of sugar cane cuttings are in the foreground.

28 Hostelry on Montserrat

Thirty miles south of Antigua is the real escapist paradise – Montserrat, one of the friendliest island dots in the Caribbean. It was presumably settled by Irish colonizers, in 1630, evidence of which is retained in the Iris lilt with which the natives speak. A volcanic mountain peak, La Soufrière (Sulphur Mountain), green hillside farms, beaches of black or white sand, and the isolated location attract tourists trying to get away from it all. As on most of the sunshine islands of the West Indies, there are good tourist accommodations on Montserrat.

29 Guadeloupe: Place de L'Église, Pointe-à-Pitre

This dignified place in the heart of old Pointe-à-Pitre is named after the stately Roman Catholic church, built in Colonial style in this quiet section of the otherwise busy city. The church is often called "The Iron Cathedral," because it is constructed of pieces of iron crisscrossed and bolted together to fortify it against hurricanes and earthquakes.

30 Guadeloupe: View from Gosier

From the dining terrace of La Pergola, a beautiful scene opens over the ocean to Basse-Terre and its high mountains, covered with dense tropical rain forests. Visible in the foreground is part of the fine beach around Gosier.

31 St. Barthélemy: The Capital, Gustavia

The beautiful island of St. Barthélemy (usually known as St. Barts) is more than 100 miles north of Guadeloupe, to which it belongs politically as a dependency. The island measures only eight square miles and has exquisite beaches and a lush tropical growth.
For almost 100 years (1784 to 1877) this typical French island belonged to Sweden. The capital, Gustavia, was developed by the Swedes and named after their king, Gustavus III. The picture shows part of the harbor, one of the most excellent ones in the Caribbean. St. Barthélemy can be reached by air from Guadeloupe or the nearby French-Dutch island of St. Martin.

32 Welcome to Dominica: Steel Band and Rainbow

The magically beautiful, tropically lush island of Dominica wraps a rainbow round your shoulder and serenades your arrival with steel band minstrelsy, clad in colorful native costumes. Dominica is famous for raising the delectable fruit that goes into Rose's Lime Juice. It's the home of a Carib-Indian reservation.

33 Fort-de-France, Capital of Martinique

Superbly situated, the capital is surrounded by hills, and faces the wide bay of the Caribbean Sea. This photograph was taken at Mount Calvary overlooking the city. Just to the left is the Roman Catholic Cathedral (St. Louis), built in 1895. The tower is constructed of steel, against the destruction of earthquakes, which destroyed other churches in the same location. The cathedral is in marked contrast to the many modern buildings of this important city of over 80,000 inhabitants, who live behind the blue waters of Baie of Fort-de-France.

34 Martinique: St. Pierre with Mont Pelée

This once-great city of the Caribbean, with more than 30,000 inhabitants, was completely destroyed on May 8, 1902, by the eruption of the volcano, Mont Pelée. The awesome volcano still dominates the horizon behind the present little town of about 5,000 people, mostly fishermen, who courageously rebuilt their village. The original city was built around a fort at the Roxelane River, and a newer district, Mouillage, was built along the shore. The city had theaters, a tramway, and the finest of harbor facilities. Today it is a quiet little village with interesting ruins and a museum containing the relics of the terrible disaster which killed every resident but one.

35 Martinique: Historic Diamond Rock

One of the great historical landmarks of the Caribbean, Diamond Rock figured in the time of Napoleon I and the war between France and England. In 1804, the British occupied "the rock" with 110 sailors and one lieutenant. The French fleet became well acquainted and quite annoyed with "the rock" over the next seventeen months, but under Boyer Peyreleau (amid almost insurmountable difficulties) the French stormed and captured it. Diamond Rock surveys the comings and goings of her people from a height of 573 feet.

36 Martinique: The Fishermen of St. Pierre

The eruption of Mont Pelée in 1902 killed every inhabitant (except one condemned prisoner who occupied a dungeon cell). Time marches on, however, and a dauntless humanity once more resides at the very edge of the buried city, building small homes over the remains and layers of ashes that cover the destroyed city.

37 St. Lucia: Countryside (Soufrière and Petit Piton)

The countryside of St. Lucia, as shown in this picture, is altogether special. Deep in the valley, right on the coast is Soufrière, the second-largest town on this beautiful island. In the background are the two peaks of the Pitons. Just behind the town is a famous volcano and bubbling sulphur springs. The therapeutic waters of these springs were originally put to use by the soldiers of Louis XVI and are still in use by sufferers of arthritic, rheumatic, and other ailments.

38 St. Lucia: Harbor of Castries

Flanked by two hills, Castries has one of the loveliest harbors and best yacht anchorages in the Caribbean, and is a favorite port of call for cruise ships. Only a few minutes from town is beautiful Vigie Beach, whose strand of white sands extends for more than three miles.

39 Barbados: Bridgetown, The Careenage

One of the landmarks of Barbados is this colorful inlet with its busy wharfs where, for over three hundred years, ships of all makes and origins have docked for overhauling, cleaning, and calking. The scene is changing fast: old buildings are replaced by new ones, and in a few years it will all be very different. This is one of the most picturesque points in the Caribbean.

40 Barbados: Dunes and Beach

Barbados, so typically English in appearance, is quite distinguishable from other Caribbean islands. There are no wild mountains here and no volcanos. Just friendly hills, covered with sugar cane and topped by plantations and churches. There are beautiful beaches all around the island, which, in addition to the excellent hotel accommodations offered here, are the greatest asset to tourism. The picture shows Crane Beach on the southeastern Atlantic coast.

41 Barbados: The Coast of St. James (Sandy Lane)

Sandy Lane is in the heart of St. James's Parish, which is the "Platinum Coast" of Barbados. The magnificent resort, built in 1961, lies directly on the beach shown in the picture. Every modern convenience and resort feature, including a nine-hole golf course, is found here.

42 Barbados: Codrington College

Christopher Codrington, founder of this seminary, was born in Barbados in 1668. In 1700 he became governor of the Leeward Islands, retiring to Barbados in 1707, where he died on Good Friday, April 7, 1710. He left his two sugar estates to the Society for the Propagation of the Gospel, in London, to be used for the founding of a college for the study of religion and medicine, under vows of chastity, poverty, and obedience, on the lines of a monastic order. Anglican priests of the Community of the Resurrection in Mirfield (Yorkshire) keep up this work in affiliation with the University of Durham (England).

43 St. Vincent: View from Sugar Mill Inn near Kingstown

Part British, part French, and altogether West Indian in local color and scenic magnificence is the tiny island of St. Vincent. Its capital, Kingstown, is renowned for its lovely English homes, and its Botanical Gardens are the oldest in the West Indies. Comfortable Sugar Mill Inn was created on the ruins of an old sugar mill.

44 Grenada – the Harbor of St. George's

Grenada is one of the most beautiful scenic islands of the West Indies. Its capital, St. George's, is situated on a craggy peninsula spectacularly colorful with red-and-white houses, green hills, and the azure waters of the harbor. Its streets are almost medievally narrow and twisting. Government offices now occupy Fort George, which was built in 1705 by the French. Just south of the city is Grand Anse, Grenada's famous beach.

45 Bequia: Princess Margaret Beach – The Grenadines

All of six square miles constitute the island of Bequia, one of the islands composing the group called The Grenadines. The exact number of these islands is not known, but they are estimated at about six hundred. Bequia is only a short distance by boat from St. Vincent and has some of the most attractive white sand beaches in the Caribbean.

46 Trinidad: Steel Band

Steel band music is fast becoming part of the folklore of Trinidad – and the Caribbean. As a musical culture, it could only have originated in a land composed of many racial and national differences living in unity, since it represents the musical culture of many peoples. Although the basic drum rhythm was introduced from Africa, it has been tempered by Western and Oriental rhythms and East Indian dance themes. Originally, the "beat" was carried by a bass bamboo drum; on one occasion an empty gas tank – or "pan," as it is called – was fortuitously substituted, and ultimately the first steel band was born. The man who brought the steel band from social nonacceptance to the threshold of respectability was Ellie Manette. Pans, by this time, had developed into instruments made of 44-gallon oil drums. Steel band players play with all the concentration, devotion, and training of a concert pianist, and there is considerable merit in the claim that these players have evolved a new tonal scale.

47 Trinidad: Hosein, the Moslem Celebration

Hosein, as the Moslems celebrate it, is not to be confused with the lighthearted festivities of Carnival. It is a celebration of religious origin, attracting many spectators with the dancing of the "moons" and the spectacular tadgeahs.

The time of Hosein celebration depends on the lunar year of the Moslem calendar; it starts with the appearance of the new moon in the month of Mohurram. Hosein commemorates the martyrdom of two princes of Islam; the tadgeahs symbolize their tombs, looking like colorful temples made of cardboard and paper.

48   Trinidad: Santa Cruz Valley

The picture looks down into fertile Santa Cruz Valley from the top of the Saddle, a pass less than ten miles north of Port-of-Spain. This is one of the richest agricultural areas of Trinidad, with many banana and citrus plantations.

49   Tobago: Tropical Wonderland

Can you picture Robinson Crusoe in these surroundings? Well, Tobagonians believe that Daniel Defoe had their romantic little tropical island in mind when he created his masterpiece. Here you will find lots of small sandy beaches set in coves or half-moon bays. The visitor succumbs almost too easily to Tobago's sun-drenched attractions, the tropical vegetation, and particularly the exotic birds living here.

50   On a Caribbean Island Schooner

The visits made to the small islands on local schooners are unforgettable. As you sail over blue Caribbean waters confident of the boating mastery of your native West Indian captain, the enchantment of the Caribbean area becomes more vivid.

51   Scarborough: Capital of Tobago

Streets and lanes and colorful houses mount the hillside of Scarborough. The houses, in particular, seem to stay put in defiance of the laws of gravity. Perched above the city is colonial Fort George, where you are able to

view capital, bay, beaches, and countryside. Trinidad, twenty-one miles southwest, is plainly visible.

52–55   Bonaire: Native Flamingo Colony

The second-largest of the ABC islands (Aruba, Bonaire, Curaçao), Bonaire, has one impressive attraction that no other island in the Caribbean can boast of. Big flocks of flamingos breed in the island's great salt lake. Easily frightened, they are difficult to photograph in their natural sanctuary. The photographer spent an entire night here, noiselessly awaiting the break of day to catch these scenes. Note the eggs in the foreground of one picture. Flamingo fledglings are first gray and turn pink only as they grow into adults.

56   Curaçao: Heerenstraat in the Business Center of Willemstad

No doubt the most colorful shopping street in Willemstad is Heerenstraat, in Punda, with its line of more or less expensive and elegant shops carrying merchandise from all over the world. The largest camera store in Curaçao, El Globo, has its headquarters here and has outstanding bargains in photographic equipment. Heerenstraat is one of the oldest streets in Willemstad, going back to approximately 1700 under the same name.

57   Curaçao: The "Floating Market," Willemstad

Along De Ruyterkade on Waaigat in Willemstad is the "Floating Market," where visiting schooners from the South American mainland and neighboring islands offer fruit, vegetables, and handicrafts for sale. The merchandise is sold directly from the ships. The sails and other material are used as awnings to cover the goods and to protect them against the sun and rain.

58   Air view of Willemstad, Capital of Curaçao

Uniquely Dutch and definitely European is the city of Willemstad. In the photograph you will note that the famous Pontoon Bridge has been opened to allow the passage of a large ocean liner. In the foreground, an old colonial fortress has been converted into a modern resort hotel of imposing dimensions. It accommodates an ever-increasing number of visitors, who come to Curaçao for pleasure and business.

59 The Bluest Waters of the Caribbean Surround Aruba

Aruba is one of the perfect holiday islands of the Caribbean, complete with luxury hotels, sparkling white sand beaches, excellent restaurants, and free-port shopping. Pictured beside the amazingly azure waters are native cactus plants and the famed *Aloe vera*, noted for its medicinal powers in the treatment of burns and cuts. This plant grows abundantly on the island.

60 Aruba: Ancient Indian Pottery

Before the arrival of the white man, Aruba was populated by friendly Indians. The Indians left many relics of their primitive culture, such as the pottery and stone ax pictured here. The Indians were not exterminated here, as they were by the Spanish on other islands. On the contrary, the island was considered by the Spanish, English, and Dutch as something of an Indian reservation. This policy resulted in amicable race relations, and Arubans today are mixture of the Indian, Spanish, and Dutch blood of the early colonists.

61 Leeward Coast of Aruba

This is a beautiful stretch of white sand beach on the leeward (west) coast of Aruba, with lush tropical vegetation. Here are the luxury hotels of Aruba–the Aruba Caribbean and the Aruba Sheraton–their spacious pool terraces, and magnificent gardens. On the same coast, farther east, is the new Manchebo Beach Hotel, built directly on the beach. To the west is Aruba's oldest beach hotel, the charming and informal Basi Ruti.

62 Sunset on Grand Cayman

The sun descends in a blaze of glory over this island that time forgot. Grand Cayman is a sportsman's island, particularly if he likes fishing, swimming, sailing, snorkeling, spearfishing, lobster progging, or wild-duck hunting. And there are beautiful beaches and good hotels.

THE PICTURES